Disasters

Events and Moments that Changed the World

Richard Whitaker

NEW
HOLLAND

First published in Australia in 2007 by
New Holland Publishers (Australia) Pty Ltd
Sydney • Auckland • London • Cape Town

1/66 Gibbes Street Chatswood NSW 2067 Australia
218 Lake Road Northcote Auckland New Zealand
86 Edgware Road London W2 2EA United Kingdom
80 McKenzie Street Cape Town 8001 South Africa

A record of this book is available from the National Library of Australia.

ISBN 9781741105636

Publisher: Fiona Schultz
Designer: Anthony Bushelle Graphics
Production Manager: Linda Bottari
Printer: Everbest Printing Company Ltd., China

10 9 8 7 6 5 4 3 2 1

Picture Credits
All images courtesy of Getty images except for Corbis p.103 and p.193
AAP p. 166

To be ignorant of what happened before you were born is to be ever a child. For what is man's lifetime unless the memory of past events is woven with those of earlier times?

Cicero (106 BC—43 BC), Orator

Disasters, Events and Moments that Changed the World starts with the Big Bang and goes right through to Hurricane Katrina in the 2005. In between it includes all the major natural disasters, great accidents and stirring moments that have became a part of world history.

Following the success of Richard Whitaker's previous book *Natural Disasters*, this book features over 60 entries and hundreds of photographs to provide a fascinating overview of the momentous events in the history of the world.

Richard Whitaker has been a meteorologist for 30 years and is the author of several books, including *All About the Weather* in the Young Reed series and an upcoming book on climate change.
He lives in Sydney, Australia.

Back cover quote: Wilhelm von Humboldt (1767—1835)

Contents

Introduction

This book looks at some of the defining events of history—the disasters, cataclysms and inspirations that helped shape the world and its various societies. The stories cover all scales of existence, ranging from the cataclysmic to the comparatively minor.

From its very beginnings an endless string of adversities has threatened life on Earth, occasionally pushing it to the verge of total oblivion. It's suspected that a massive meteorite impact with our planet some 65 million years ago may have ended the reign of the dinosaurs and wiped out up to 75 per cent of all species. But life clawed its way back to recolonise the Earth and led eventually to the beginnings of the human race.

The arrival of humanity had amazing consequences for the planet. Human beings rapidly rose to the apex of the animal kingdom, and to this day dominate the scene like no other species ever has. This is despite humans' comparatively fragile physique and their lack of well-developed weaponry such as claws and fangs that enable other animals to survive in an often hostile environment. Humans use 'intelligence' to overcome their physical shortcomings, with spectacular success. Paradoxically, this fantastic intelligence has not always enabled humankind to live in harmony, either with the environment or among themselves. History is riddled with periods of warfare between various human groups; during twentieth century conflicts, millions were killed by weapons that had become increasingly deadly.

Mankind has also been directly involved in the total elimination of many plant and animal species; other species, such as the American buffalo and the Australian bilby, were rescued from the brink of extinction only at the eleventh hour.

In addition, humanity has faced global outbreaks of disease, natural disasters such as volcanic eruptions, earthquakes and extreme weather, as well as famine and climate change. Such events have wiped from existence entire civilisations such as the Sumerian and the Minoan. Yet new populations have always risen to take their place.

Much smaller scale events have also played a role in the way humans interact with each other and in the evolution of our laws. Crime, and our attempts to deal with it, is part of the human story, as are racism, politics, finance, sport and invention.

In this book we look at just a handful of events from the vast pool of history. These events changed sometimes the whole world, sometimes just a part of it, because of their huge physical impact or significant social consequence. This virtual diorama of existence becomes a mirror in which we see ourselves moving towards an uncertain future, but a future determined by the infinite resilience of the Earth and of the human spirit, which has always triumphed over tragedy.

Above all, despite the incredible adversity that has had to be confronted throughout history, and will continue to oppose us in the future, this is a story of optimism, as the Earth and the plant and animal species that populate it evolve to face each new challenge and adapt to the continuously changing circumstances of existence.

Defining moments in history: the terrorist murders of Israeli athletes at the Munich Olympics brought the Middle East crisis into the living rooms of the world (see page 194).

Lemaître and Hubble showed
that far from being the entire
universe, the Milky Way was
only one of countless galaxies
in a universe that stretched
away almost beyond the limit
of human comprehension.

A Hubble Telescope view of the Universe showing far distant galaxies moving away from Earth.

The Big Bang

Humanity's view of the universe has changed enormously over time. Up until the Middle Ages it was generally believed in Europe that the universe was a closed space bounded by a spherical envelope, beyond which there was a complete vacuum containing no matter or energy of any sort. Earth was the central point of this universe, and the sun, together with the other celestial bodies, revolved around it.

The early Polish astronomer Nicolaus Copernicus (1473–1543) famously challenged this viewpoint when he published his *De Revolutionibus* in 1530. In this treatise he asserts that Earth and other planets revolved around the Sun, a theory that received the strong endorsement of the famous Italian Galileo Galilei (1564–1642). This was to the great displeasure of the Roman Catholic Church, however, which considered the idea to be heretical and to contravene the teachings of the Scriptures.

Nonetheless, over the next four hundred years, Copernicus's ideas were generally adopted by astronomers. They became a cornerstone of a gradually evolving model of the universe that increasingly intrigued scientists of all persuasions.

Until the early nineteenth century it was believed that the entire cosmos consisted of the Milky Way galaxy, and that this had existed 'forever' in much the same way as it appeared now. But in the 1920s, in much the same way that Copernicus had jolted the astronomical status quo of the Middle Ages, a Belgian priest George Lemaitre and a young American astronomer Edwin Hubble proposed a bold new theory. They showed that far from being the entire universe, the Milky Way was only one of countless galaxies in a universe that stretched away almost beyond the limit of human comprehension.

Hubble also put forward the radical notion that the universe was 'flying apart'; this explained a strange phenomenon called the 'red shift'— the observation that light from distant galaxies appears 'redder' than expected. When a light-emitting object moves away from us, the light appears to shift to the red end of the spectrum, and when approaching us, to the blue end. A rapidly expanding universe would explain the red shift that scientists actually observe.

Later discoveries helped refine Lemaitre and Hubble's theory into the so-called 'Big Bang' theory, which today is the dominant explanation of the origin of the universe. This suggests that 10 to 20 billion years ago all of the matter and energy in existence was concentrated in one infinitesimally small point until an apocalyptic explosion hurled matter in all directions. This matter eventually clumped together to form the galaxies, which continue to speed outward, away from the centre of the explosion.

The theory gained massive credence when none other than the great physicist Albert Einstein stated that the 'Big Bang' was consistent with his theory of relativity. And, unlike Galileo's experience, various church groups also enthusiastically embraced the idea, as it seemed to suggest a moment of creation, as noted in the Scriptures.

Although the most plausible explanation of the origin of the universe thus far, the 'Big Bang' theory leaves several fundamental questions unanswered; for instance, why was all matter and energy concentrated at a pinpoint in the first place, and what triggered the unbelievably large explosion?

The theory is under constant review and is being continuously re-evaluated in the light of further scientific discoveries, but it has stood the test of time well. The 'Big Bang' remains one of science's most famous and popular theories.

A scorching vapour cloud surged across North America, obliterating everything in its path, including most of the life forms, both plant and animal, that had developed over the previous few million years.

An artist's impression of an ancient dinosaur called Guanlong Wucaii, the oldest known species of tyrannosaurus.

The End of the Dinosaurs

The end of the dinosaur dynasty has long fascinated scientists. Various theories have been proposed to explain what appears to have been a rapid mass extinction around 65 million years ago.

Much of the available evidence comes from a geological layer called the K-T boundary. In the nineteenth century, geologists investigating fossil evidence from Earth's early history realised that there was quite a sharp geological boundary between the Cretaceous period (135 to 65 million years ago) and the Tertiary period (65 million years ago to the present). This became known as the K-T boundary, from K, the abbreviation for Kreide, 'chalk', used in German to refer to the Cretaceous, and T for Tertiary.

In several areas around the world, rocks deposited during the two periods are separated by a thin layer of clay that has an extraordinarily high concentration of the element iridium, which is comparatively rare on Earth. Astronomers were aware that iridium is much more abundant in meteorites, asteroids and comets than on Earth, and this led to the theory that a massive impact with some type of extraterrestrial object might have caused the mass extinction of the dinosaurs.

Further investigation suggested that around the time of the genesis of the K-T boundary, not only the dinosaurs disappeared, but also a staggering 75 per cent of the entire species existing on the planet at the time, including the vast majority of planktonic life in the oceans.

The obvious question arose: if there had been some sort of cataclysmic collision between a comet or asteroid and Earth, where was the impact point? Intensive research by geologists culminated in the discovery of a massive crater, partly submerged, along the southern shore of the Gulf of Mexico, and a stunning picture of one of the major defining moments in the history of Earth emerged.

It is thought that one day, around 65 million years ago, a massive asteroid about 10 kilometres across tore through our atmosphere and smashed into what is now the Yucatan Peninsula of Mexico with unimaginable violence.

Normally, 'space rocks' entering our atmosphere tend to slow down because of air resistance and then begin to burn up and fall to the ground under the influence of gravity. Often they vaporise before reaching the surface; sometimes they fall across the ground as a comparatively harmless shower of small pebbles. But a massive body such as a large asteroid, travelling at around 258 000 kilometres an hour would only be slightly impeded by the atmosphere and would reach the Earth's surface at very high speed.

The Yucatan impact was in this category. It blasted a monstrous crater in Earth's surface, upwards of 160 kilometres across, and catapulted a vast cloud of earth and rock debris high into the upper levels of the atmosphere.

A scorching vapour cloud surged across North America, obliterating everything in its path, including most of the life forms, both plant and animal, that had developed over the previous few million years.

The massive dust cloud produced by the explosion encircled Earth, blocking out the Sun's rays and causing a sharp cooling of the global temperature regime. Plants, and the animals that depended on them, began to die off, including most of the dinosaurs that had dominated the scene for the previous 100 million years.

It is believed that many species, both land based and marine, were entirely eliminated by this 'Armageddon' event and Earth was only slowly repopulated by the evolution of new species over the following millennia.

The Great Flood

7:17 *And the flood was forty days upon the earth; and the waters increased, and bore up the ark, and it was lift up above the earth.*

7:23 *And every living substance was destroyed which was upon the face of the ground, both man, and cattle, and the creeping things, and the fowl of the heaven; and they were destroyed from the earth: and Noah only remained alive, and they that were with him in the ark.*

7:24 *And the waters prevailed upon the earth an hundred and fifty days.*

The Book of Genesis

The fabulous story of Noah and the ark appears in the Book of Genesis in the Old Testament and has been the subject of considerable debate down the centuries. Modern-day cynics claim that there is little or no historical evidence for the Great Flood and that a global inundation is scientifically impossible anyway, as there is not enough water in the atmospheric system to create such a catastrophe. But there is also widespread acceptance that a great inundation did occur across the Middle Eastern region around this time, undoubtedly accompanied by widespread destruction and loss of life. Several fruitless attempts have been made to locate the final resting place of the ark, believed by many to be modern-day Mount Ararat in Turkey.

Interestingly, the story of a massive flood appears in several early historical accounts and forms part of Jewish, Christian and Muslim traditions, being mentioned in the Qur'an as well as the Old Testament. Early references to a devastating flood across the Middle East and the countries of the eastern Mediterranean can be found in Mesopotamian writings of around 2000 BC, and in a Sumerian account of approximately 1700 BC found on a clay stone known as the Nippur Tablet. It would appear that the Old Testament account was derived from these earlier references, as there is a great deal in common among all the writings.

…God became increasingly disgusted with the sins of humankind and decided to destroy all life on Earth, apart from a select group that would be permitted to start again.

The story in Genesis tells that God became increasingly disgusted with the sins of humankind and decided to destroy all life on Earth, apart from a select group that would be permitted to start again. He ordered his faithful servant Noah to construct a great boat—the ark—according to quite specific details.

It was to be made of cypress, 300 cubits long, 50 cubits wide and 30 cubits high. (The cubit was an ancient measure of length taken from the elbow to the tip of the longest finger of a man and corresponds to around 46 centimetres.) In modern terms the ark would have been about 138 metres long, 23 metres wide and 21 metres high—roughly half the size of the *Titanic*.

Upon completion, Noah was to take his family aboard, including his wife, his sons and their wives, along with 'two of all living creatures, male and female', from which the next generation of Earth's animals would be born.

After this was done, tremendous rains fell for forty days and forty nights, producing a vast flood that wiped out all known life apart from that aboard the Ark, which floated across the land on the floodwaters. Finally the flood began to abate and as the waters receded, the ark settled on a mountain top, allowing its passengers—human and animal—to disembark and begin a new existence.

An artist's impression of Noah gathering the animals two by two.

The ark floats on the waters of the Great Flood.

Ancient Sumerian ruins built by King Gilgamesh around 4700 years ago.

The Collapse of Sumer

One of the oldest civilisations known, Sumer flourished over six thousand years ago, well before the golden age of early Egypt. Ancient Sumer lay across what is now much of modern-day Iraq, including Baghdad, and consisted of twelve separate walled city-states, each with common religious, architectural and political features.

The cities were surrounded by villages and farms serviced by irrigation systems constructed to take water from the Tigris and Euphrates rivers, making the Sumerians probably the first in history to use advanced and highly organised agricultural techniques.

In addition, they invented seeding equipment with which to sow their crops and achieved crop yields on a similar or even superior scale of those produced in medieval Europe some five thousand years later. The food supply became so that the population of Sumer reached an estimated one million people at the height of its power.

Many of the elements of modern civilisation can be traced back to ancient Sumer. The custom of measuring time in units of 60 (60 seconds to a minute, 60 minutes to an hour) is a Sumerian one; Sumerian priests also divided the circle into 360 degrees, or six lots of 60.

The Sumerians also studied astronomy, engaged in international trade, were the first people to produce a written language (cuneiform text), composed music and produced advanced, stylistic art. Their impact on the ancient world was immense and has continued to modern times.

This highly successful, even dazzling, civilisation began to decline after an existence of around two thousand years. It's generally believed that there were two main reasons for this. Firstly, there was the continued aggressive incursions of the Amorites—nomadic tribes of herders who forced their way into any areas suitable for grazing their herds—and secondly, a loss of agricultural productivity.

The Amorites seem to have been ferocious warriors, with one Biblical account noting: 'Then the Amorites who lived in that hill country came out against you and chased you as bees do and beat you down in Se'ir as far as Hormah' (Deuteronomy 1:44). They are described as a large and physically powerful people, with the bed of their king, Og, recorded as being a giant nine cubits (4.1 metres) in length, and four cubits (1.8 metres) wide.

At first the Amorite incursions were only nuisance to Sumer, but repeated invasions over centuries eventually took their toll and substantially weakened the empire. It has been suggested that the Amorite attacks combined with a more insidious enemy—salinity —to jointly bring about the collapse of Sumer. Ironically, irrigation—one of the main reasons for the great success of the civilisation—may also have brought about its downfall.

Accounts written on the cuneiform tablets of the day suggest that the once fertile valleys in which the Sumerians grew such great crops for many centuries became less and less productive. The form of irrigation they used involved draining water from the rivers into low-lying surrounding land where it was left to percolate into the soil. After centuries of this it is likely that deeply embedded ground salts rose to the surface and contaminated the soil. Interestingly, the same form of contamination is taking place today in many modern-day irrigation projects, resulting in severe degradation of the land.

> The Sumerians also studied astronomy, engaged in international trade, were the first people to produce a written language (cuneiform text), composed music and produced advanced, stylistic art.

Ruins of the Palace of Knossos, a Minoan structure on the island of Crete.

The End of the Minoans

One of the greatest of the early Mediterranean civilisations was all but lost to history until late in the nineteenth century, when the English archaeologist Sir Arthur Evans excavated a number of spectacular ruins on the island of Crete.

Realising that his team had discovered relics of an early civilisation, which revealed distinctive architecture, art, technology and religion, Evans called it the Minoan civilisation, after the mythical king Minos of early Cretan history.

Over the years archaeological studies revealed the existence of an astonishing, highly advanced mercantile culture extending from about 3000 to 1200 BC. Minoans actively traded with nearby countries, including Greece, Egypt, Spain and Syria. In marked contrast to their neighbours at the time, they were generally peaceful and non-warlike. There is little evidence for any sort of military hierarchy, and archaeologists have noted that Minoan weapons as depicted in some of their art seem more ceremonial in nature than utilitarian.

Minoan religion was dominated by the worship of a series of goddesses, whom it was believed controlled all aspects of society, including fertility, cities, harvests and the animals. The existence of a well-developed written language was evident from numerous inscribed clay tablets discovered around the excavations. Although many have never been 'decoded', most appear to be trade related—records and inventories of goods and services. The Minoans were also advanced agriculturalists, using oxen to plough the fields and sowing such crops as wheat and barley, as well as raising domestic animals, including cattle, pigs, goats and sheep.

After thriving for over 1500 years, the Minoan cities went into a decline, with several theories being proposed to explain this. There seems little doubt that the major factor was a massive eruption of the volcanic island of Thera, site of present-day Santorini, about 1650 BC; one of the largest volcanic cataclysms in the last ten millennia, it has been extensively studied by vulcanologists.

Santorini lies only about 70 kilometres from Crete. It's thought that an unimaginably violent explosion triggered a massive collapse of the volcano, with millions of tonnes of rock and magma falling into the sea. This would probably have generated a massive tsunami that descended on Crete only minutes later. Such an event might well have wiped out many coastal settlements as well as most of the ships that formed the backbone of the Minoan maritime trade structure. A colossal ash canopy would also have been produced, perhaps resulting in volcanic winters and poor harvests right across the Mediterranean for several years to follow.

Another factor in the demise of the Minoans may well have been the invasion of the Mycenaeans when, some two hundred years after the eruption, they occupied and later settled Crete. The peaceful Minoans would have been easy prey for the aggressive and warlike Mycenaeans. Whatever the causes, the decline of the Minoan civilisation accelerated and their distinctive society apparently died out around 1200 BC.

The memory of this advanced but gentle society gradually faded and its fabulous cities were slowly covered by the detritus of the passing centuries. It was not until another three thousand years had passed that the shovels of Sir Arthur Evans' archaeological team revealed them to the sunlight once again.

> After thriving for over 1500 years, the Minoan cities went into a decline, with several theories being proposed to explain this.

The Decline of the Roman Empire

It is difficult to say exactly when the Roman Empire fell—rather than a single cataclysmic event, it appears that numerous developments produced a gradual weakening of what was arguably the greatest of all the ancient civilisations.

Ironically, it can also be argued that Rome itself never fell—it's alive and well today. However, there is little doubt that it shrank to only a shadow of its former self around the fifth century. During this dark period, it was transformed from a thriving metropolis with a large population to a mere provincial settlement of several thousand, surrounded by swampland.

There has always been great discussion about what led to this decline, but it is now seen as an ongoing process that lasted for well over a hundred years, with roots going back several centuries. Diverse factors have been blamed for the progressive erosion of Rome's strengths:

- The Roman legions' continuous need for young men to fight in wars all around the ancient world depleted the essential labour force from family farms, weakening the rural population.
- Increasingly aggressive incursions of several northern and central European 'barbarian' tribes, such as the Goths, Huns and Vandals, increased pressure on the Roman army and led directly to the 'division' of the Empire. This occurred when Constantine, who ruled from 323 to 337, chose to leave Rome and rule the empire from Byzantium (which he renamed Constantinople), and this division spread the military protection provided by the army much more thinly.

- Rome's citizens were experiencing declining health, possibly as a result of lead poisoning (the city's water supply was carried through lead pipes).

In recent times DNA analysis of the bones of Roman children from the Lugano area, dating from around 450 AD, revealed the presence of malaria—perhaps the explanation of the 'Roman fever' referred to in historical texts. Persistent outbreaks of malaria across central Italy during this period could well have had a devastating effect on the general population.

By the sixth century, Rome had sunk into a state of complete disrepair: the ancient palaces were plundered, schools were destroyed and roads and bridges were overgrown with vegetation. It was to be many centuries before the city was able to recover and again become one of the world's great metropolises.

> By the sixth century, Rome had sunk into a state of complete disrepair: the ancient palaces were plundered, schools were destroyed and roads and bridges were overgrown with vegetation.

The Colosseum

Without doubt one of the most famous and well-known ancient structures still in existence, the Colosseum illustrates the great contradictions of ancient Rome. Its fabulous, almost modern architecture, as well as the amazingly advanced engineering, make it one of the most significant surviving structures of the ancient world. However, it is also—at least by modern standards—a terrible monument to the extreme cruelty and depravity of the times.

Chariot racing in the Colosseum circa 248 AD.

Originally known as the Flavian Amphitheatre, it was completed in 80 AD, and provided seating for a vast crowd of 50 000 people, comparing well with most modern stadiums. Its advanced design meant that it could empty of people in around five minutes. Beneath the wooden floor of the main arena was a great labyrinth of rooms and passageways for the containment of wild beasts, gladiators and 'props' used for the general entertainment.

It was the site of unparalleled cruelty for around four hundred years, during which time thousands of slaves, captive enemies, gladiators and beasts slaughtered each other for the amusement of the general population.

Julius Caesar (102 – 44BC) invades Britain.

A relief from the Arch of Constantine in Rome, circa 400 AD depicting a cavalry charge.

Vesuvius exploded with phenomenal violence, shooting a column of ash some 32 kilometres into the atmosphere and ejecting vast quantities of ash and rock from its crater.

Ruins of Pompeii showing a public drinking fountain in the foreground.

The Eruption of Mount Vesuvius

One of the most famous cataclysms ever recorded, the eruption of Mount Vesuvius in 79 AD changed the course of history: it wiped out two of the great cities of Antiquity, which were then forgotten, only to be rediscovered some 1700 years later.

Mount Vesuvius is an active and dangerous volcano located near the coast on the Bay of Naples in Italy. It has erupted on 36 occasions over the last 2000 years, most recently in 1944. Some eruptions have been so explosive that much of southern Europe has been coated in ash, on at least two occasions affecting Istanbul, over 1600 kilometres away.

However, it was the apocalyptic eruption in 79 that left an indelible mark on the history books. The trouble appears to have begun with a series of powerful earthquakes in the year 62, which continued intermittently over the next seventeen years. This did not cause any particular concern to the local citizens, as earth tremors were common across the area. But in this case they were portents of catastrophe.

On 24 August 79, Vesuvius exploded with phenomenal violence, shooting a column of ash some 32 kilometres into the atmosphere and ejecting vast quantities of ash and rock from its crater.

The surreal scenes that followed were famously described by the Roman writer Pliny the Younger, an actual observer of the drama. He wrote of the eruptive cloud:

I cannot give you a more exact description of its figure, than by resembling it to that of a pine tree; for it shot up to a great height in the form of a tall trunk, which spread out at the top into a sort of branches. It appeared sometimes bright, and sometimes dark and spotted, as it was either more or less impregnated with earth and cinders.

From Pliny's Epistulae 1–9

Avalanches of superheated volcanic gases containing hot ash and rock fragments cascaded down the mountainside and spread out at the base, travelling many kilometres and overwhelming everything in their path. This phenomenon is called a pyroclastic flow; internal temperatures can exceed 600°C, with the cloud spreading out at more than 160 kilometres per hour. The city of Herculaneum, only about 1.6 kilometres from the crater, was almost immediately obliterated, followed by Pompeii, located a little further away from the eruption. It's estimated that about 10 000 people were killed in the two cities, which were buried under several metres of ash and volcanic stones.

As the centuries rolled past, the memories of Pompeii and Herculaneum gradually faded into oblivion and succeeding generations walked across the ground and worked the area, entirely unaware of the dead cities below them.

They were finally rediscovered towards the middle of the eighteenth century, and since then the world has been entranced by the treasure trove of ancient Roman relics recovered and so well preserved by the ash that had caused the disaster. Plaster poured into cavities left by incinerated bodies beneath the solidified ash blanket has produced near-perfect moulds of the people and animals that perished in the disaster, and has added a tragic dimension to the excavations.

Today Pompeii is the most popular tourist destination in Italy with an estimated two million visitors flocking to the site every year.

The Invention of Gunpowder

The invention of gunpowder in ancient China seems to have been motivated by the desire to produce spectacular special effects as a background for public ceremonies, leading to the further refinement into fireworks.

Early oriental alchemists could not have foreseen the developments that were to take place over the next few hundred years, when their curious invention would be continuously refined to produce military weapons that would ultimately kill millions of people. Gunpowder would also reshape civilisation, for it offered immense military superiority to technologically advanced cultures over barbarian armies, and massive castles and fortifications became progressively less important.

The early Chinese had discovered that if powdered sulphur was mixed with charcoal and set alight it burnt vigorously. Around 850, in a crucial step forward, potassium nitrate (saltpetre) crystals were added to the mixture, producing an explosive reaction when ignited.

Furthermore, if this mixture was placed in a closed environment, such as inside a length of bamboo with one end sealed, the resulting explosion would be directed towards the open end with much greater force than if the explosion took place in the open. This was naturally of interest to the military, and by the twelfth century some of the Chinese armies had added to their arsenals bombs and rockets powered by this explosive powder.

It was only a matter of time before someone got the idea of inserting a projectile in the open end of the bamboo, and by the early twelfth century the Chinese had also produced a crude cannon that fired a flaming missile towards the enemy. It was soon realised that if the barrel were made of metal instead of bamboo, a heavier charge could be used, throwing a projectile faster and further.

The news of this exciting technology soon spread west over the ancient trade route called the Silk Road, enabling the Arabs to manufacture crude firearms by the end of the twelfth century. The technology spread across Europe, where early cannons appeared in the thirteenth century.

Initially the military reasoned that bigger was better, and monstrous iron cannons designed to knock down the walls and ramparts of stone castles appeared on the battlefield. These weapons were cumbersome, crude and dangerous, frequently exploding and killing their own gun crews.

The production of lighter, stronger barrels made of bronze instead of iron, and improvements in the manufacturing process of the gunpowder itself, producing a more stable and powerful explosive mixture, greatly improved effectiveness and lessened the risk to those who operated the cannons.

Cannons were initially seen as a replacement for the ancient catapults and trebuchets. But it was eventually discovered that small hand-held weapons carried by individual soldiers and powered by gunpowder could fire small

> It was only a matter of time before someone got the idea of inserting a projectile in the open end of the bamboo, and by the early twelfth century the Chinese had also produced a crude cannon that fired a flaming missile towards the enemy.

An early cannon used at the Battle of Crecy in 1346.

projectiles at the enemy with even more devastating results.

Refinements to the manufacture of gunpowder and associated weaponry continued to be made throughout the Middle Ages (1400–1700) and well into the nineteenth century. Gunpowder was gradually replaced by more powerful and safer explosives such as melinite, lyddite and cordite.

The last major military action fought with gunpowder as the propellant for artillery was the Spanish-American War of 1898. Gunpowder continues to be used in time-fuses, fireworks and signals.

The Crusades

The Crusades were an early example of what has been a recurrent theme in history ever since—warfare caused by religious differences. And just as we see today, the specific object of dispute was the Holy Land (now called Israel), including the city of Jerusalem, sacred to both Christians and Muslims.

Islam took control of Jerusalem from the Byzantine Empire in the early seventh century, but permitted Christians to continue making pilgrimages there for the next four hundred years. During the eleventh century, Jerusalem was taken over by the Seljuk Turks who instead of maintaining the status quo locked the city down and banned all Christian pilgrimages.

This precipitated a series of intermittent wars between Christians and Muslims that lasted nearly two centuries and was responsible for the slaughter of tens of thousands of people. These Christian military expeditions, involving, among others, English, French, German and Italian soldiers, became known as the Crusades; they resulted in seven separate major conflicts.

Following the banning of Christians from Jerusalem, the ruling Pope, Urban II, made what has been described as one of the key speeches in the Church's history, when he urged the Christians of Europe to take up arms and march against the 'infidel Turks'.

> The West must march to the defence of the East. All should go, rich and poor alike. The Franks must stop their internal wars and squabbles. Let them go instead against the infidel and fight a righteous war.
> God himself will lead them, for they will be doing His work. There will be absolution and remission of sins for all who die in the service of Christ. Here they are poor and miserable sinners; there they will be rich and happy. Let none hesitate; they must march next summer. God wills it!
>
> Pope Urban II, Council of Clermont, 1095

The promise of a rich and happy afterlife was essential to the cause, as was the notion that this was God's work. *Deus vult* (God wills it) became the central justification for the Crusades. The symbol of the Crusaders was a red cross displayed on a white tunic, and most of the expeditions over the next 200 years received the blessing of the Papacy.

The army of the First Crusade (1096–99), consisting of soldiers from several European countries, took Jerusalem, but only after a shocking massacre of much of the population. The remaining six Crusades produced mixed results, with power seesawing between the Christian armies and the forces of Islam. Perhaps the most famous conflict from the English viewpoint was the Third Crusade (1188–92) because it involved the presence of King Richard—'Richard the Lion-Heart'—who became a central figure in British history.

The final Crusade ended in 1291, the Crusaders' loss to the Muslim forces ending almost two hundred years of bloody conflict. To the Christianised West the entire endeavour was a failure. No permanent conquest of the Holy Land was achieved, nor was the onward march of Islam halted. The relationship between Islam and Christianity was permanently marred. Even very recently, Western involvement in parts of the Middle East was on at least one occasion referred to as a crusade by US President George W. Bush.

Some good did come out of the Crusades. Parts of the high Islamic culture involving advanced knowledge of astronomy, mathematics, architecture and medicine made their way back to the West. Many of the ancient Roman roads across Europe that had fallen into disrepair were also resurrected.

Above: A naval battle involving England and France against the Saracens circa 1290.

Below: A crusader is hit with an arrow fired by a Muslim soldier, circa 1250.

The Englishman Nicholas Burton is tortured by officers of the Spanish Inquisition in Cadiz, 1560.

The Inquisition

The Inquisition, controlled by the Congregation of the Holy Office of the Roman Catholic Church, was designed to identify and then suitably punish heretics, who included anyone who failed to agree entirely with the doctrines of the Church.

It lasted for around six hundred years. The Inquisition remains a gross blot not only on the history of the Church, but also on those societies and nations of the day that allowed the atrocities associated with it to continue for so long. Many thousands were tortured, burnt at the stake, imprisoned and robbed of their possessions, usually for no valid reason whatsoever.

These despicable acts had the full backing of the secular governments of the day, as well as the approval of the general populace of many European countries. Not to approve of the sickening activities was very dangerous as this could in itself lead to charges of heresy.

The Inquisition had two main periods: the Medieval Inquisition and the Spanish Inquisition, the latter having a greater extent of government support and involvement.

The Medieval Inquisition was instituted by Pope Gregory IX in 1227, based on extremely flimsy interpretations of verses from the Old Testament. The Church had become increasingly concerned with an increase in a free-thinking, alternative interpretation of the Scriptures that it regarded as an evil.

The first inquisitors were clergy of the Dominican and Franciscan orders, teams of whom would tour the countryside, visiting villages or towns along the way. Often the head inquisitor would address the town population in the village square, inviting them to name those who were suspected of heresy. To know such a person and not to name him or her was also considered a heresy, and this policy led to father naming son, brother naming sister and a wife her husband. It needed only two accusations to initiate an investigation, with no hard evidence of any type required.

The accused was then summoned to appear before the inquisitors, to be interrogated at length and in minute detail. Interrogations were held in secret and the names of accusers were not revealed. During the time between accusation and sentence the accused would normally be imprisoned, which was often a prolonged period of several months or even years.

Every encouragement was made to persuade the accused to confess their heresy, and if this was done, lighter penalties in the form of 'penances' were imposed. These could include being forced to wear yellow crosses on clothing, further imprisonment, floggings, or enforced pilgrimages to religious shrines.

But incredibly severe penalties were imposed on those heretics who refused to recant or those who were second offenders, in the form of prolonged torture, confiscation of assets and, most horribly of all, burning at the stake.

The Spanish Inquisition (1478–1834) constituted a particularly evil version of this process, with the Grand Inquisitor, the Dominican Friar Tomás de Torquemada, notorious for his use of cruelty and extended torture.

Many thousands of people suffered under the injustices of the Inquisition over the centuries, with non-Catholic groups bearing the brunt of the terror. Protestants, Muslims and Jews were all considered heretics by definition; their only hope of survival was to renounce their religion and convert to Catholicism.

While the period spanning the Middle Ages was, at least by today's standards, a time of great ignorance and cruelty, even with that background, the Inquisition stands apart as an episode of unparalleled intolerance and barbarity.

People praying for salvation from the plague, circa 1350.

The effects of the plague in Basle, Switzerland, circa 1349.

The Black Plague

One of history's great population disasters was triggered not by a meteorite impact, not by a volcano or by deadly and extensive warfare. The culprit in this case was the oriental rat flea.

Some historians believe that the disaster originated during the 1330s with an outbreak of bubonic plague somewhere in China. This disease affects rats and is also readily transmissible to humans via the fleas that rats always carry. And, since from the earliest days of maritime trade, rats have been willing passengers aboard ships, it was only a matter of time before plague-infested rats migrated from East to West.

In those times there was no understanding of the connection between rat, flea and human that produced the deadly march of the disease. General hygiene in the big cities across Europe was poor, with refuse common in the streets and around houses, providing ideal environments for rats to breed. Personal hygiene was also poor by modern standards, and fleas and bed bugs were common household guests.

But one of the main problems was the primitive state of development of medical science at that time—once a person contracted the plague they lived or died according to chance. There was nothing medicine could do to help.

Early signs of the onset of the disease were swellings (or buboes) that appeared in the lymph glands around the armpits, neck and groin; from this point, victims often only had a week to live. During this period black spots often erupted on the skin, leading to the name 'Black Plague' used in England.

The disease affected Italy first in 1347 and then marched inexorably through Europe before launching across to the British Isles in August

Entire families were wiped out, with the surviving neighbours fleeing the area and leaving deserted homes full of dead bodies.

of 1348. The death toll mounted steadily, with hundreds of thousands dying in cities, villages and even rural areas. Entire families were wiped out, with the surviving neighbours fleeing the area and leaving deserted homes full of dead bodies.

The population of all these areas became completely panicked and with no known cause or solution turned to all manner of sorcery, quackery and cures. Many, believing that the disease came from the air, used vapours and scents to purify their households. Townfolk fired cannons and rang the village church bells constantly to try and drive the disease away. There was a thriving trade in talismans, good luck charms, potions and spells.

The grim march of the plague continued back and forth across Europe and the British Isles for the next five years, but with a noticeable decrease during winter, when fleas were dormant.

By the end of 1351, around a third of Europe's population was dead, almost 25 million people. The plague had almost run its terrible course, although further outbreaks occurred from time to time, in particular another major flare-up during the 1600s.

Europe was never to be the same again: there were major and long-lasting economic and social effects from the plague. People's faith in the Church was shaken and, because of the shortage of labour, peasants were in a position to demand higher wages. Western civilisation looked towards a new direction with the dawn of the fifteenth century.

The Death of Joan of Arc

Jeanne d'Arc (known in English-speaking countries as Joan of Arc) was one of the most remarkable women of recorded history. She was born into turbulent times during the infamous Hundred Years' War between England and France in the fifteenth century, when England was determined to attain a decisive military conquest over her old enemy.

The Hundred Years' War was in fact a series of wars, some of which were directed by the then King of England, Henry VI, in his attempt to seize control of France from the Valois Dauphin Charles VII. Charles was due to become the next King of France following the death of his father, Charles VI.

Joan was born in the Lorraine region of France in 1412, the scene of heavy fighting on several occasions during the period of conflict. She was deeply religious from a very young age, and soon after she turned thirteen heard what she believed were the voices of saints telling her that she had been chosen by God to assist Charles in driving the English out of France.

After several fruitless attempts to see Charles, who was understandably sceptical, she was eventually able to convince him of her ability and intent. This was proof of the extraordinary persuasive powers of this very young woman in the face of an all-male decision-making process.

Even more amazing was Charles' reaction—in 1429, he gave Joan command of one of the French armies. She was only seventeen years old and had no military experience. This unprecedented decision immediately paid off when she led her troops into battle against the English at Orleans: against all odds and logic, she defeated them and pushed their army into a headlong retreat. This led to the coronation of Charles as the King of France at the ancient city of Rheims later in the year—with Joan standing beside him.

After this astonishing victory, her army attacked the English in Paris but was repulsed, with Joan being wounded in the battle. Disaster struck in 1430 when she was captured by the forces of Burgundy (a French group allied to the English) and sold as a prisoner to the English.

Despite the fact that Charles owed his throne to her efforts, he made little effort to save her and she was tried in the pro-English ecclesiastical courts at Rouen, charged with sorcery, heresy and witchcraft. Found guilty, Joan was burnt at the stake as a witch before a large crowd on 30 May 1431 at Rouen. Because she was officially a heretic, her body could not be buried in consecrated ground; instead her ashes were thrown into the River Seine. She was just nineteen years old.

Over the centuries, her reputation continued to grow, and in 1920 she was canonised by Pope Benedict XV as Saint Joan of Arc. Revealing the true measure of her greatness, her old enemies, the English, came to adore her as much as the French, Sir Winston Churchill later writing that 'Joan was a being so uplifted from the ordinary run of mankind that she finds no equal in a thousand years'.

Saint Joan of Arc is now a patron saint of France and recognised internationally as one of the greatest heroines of history.

> Despite the fact that Charles owed his throne to her efforts, he made little effort to save her and she was tried in the pro-English ecclesiastical courts at Rouen, charged with sorcery, heresy and witchcraft.

Joan of Arc in armour on horseback, circa 1429.

A map of the west coast of Greenland circa 1350, with the black dots marking individual Viking settlements.

The End of the Greenland Colony

The climate of the Earth is constantly changing, with evidence from the past pointing to considerable variations in temperature and rainfall patterns across many areas. For example, in Europe, around 900 the climate began to warm considerably, at the start of an epoch lasting about 450 years. This became known as the Medieval Warm Period.

This was followed by an abrupt fall in temperatures across Europe during the 500-year period from around 1350 to 1850. This was called the 'Little Ice Age'. These major fluctuations in temperature were to have a great impact on Europe, and in particular on the 'Greenland colony', whose existence straddled the transition from the Medieval Warm Period to the Little Ice Age.

In 985, during the early stages of the Medieval Warm Period, an expedition led by the Icelandic Viking chieftain Erik the Red (so named because of his red hair), and numbering some three hundred people, made the first known European landing on the west coast of what was later to be called Greenland. In order to expand the Viking empire the group established two settlements, naming the coastal one *Eystribygg* (eastern settlement) and that further inland *Vestribygg* (western settlement), and began general farming, including the grazing of domestic livestock they had brought with them.

Conditions were in large part onerous, with the lengthy, frigid winters an annual menace. The mild summers, however, enabled the settlers to cultivate their farms and increase the sizes of their herds of cattle, sheep and goats. They also fished and hunted seal. Periodically other intrepid Vikings sailed across from Iceland, some to settle, others to return home after offloading supplies. Despite the tough life, the populations of the two settlements grew, and by the early 1100s more than three hundred farms across the area supported some three thousand people.

About this time weather conditions deteriorated, for the Little Ice Age affected Greenland well before it became obvious in Europe. Around the middle of the twelfth century, Greenland temperatures fell sharply, with prolonged periods of below freezing conditions extending into the spring and autumn, and storms increased across the region. Pack ice extended further away from the shoreline, making voyages from Iceland more difficult and less frequent, the periodic visits now often separated by many years.

The last recorded contact between the Greenland colony and the outside world occurred in 1410, and it is believed that the last inhabitants died in the late 1400s, probably as a result of malnutrition and persistently cold temperatures. It has been suggested that hostile confrontations with indigenous Inuit peoples may also have played a role, but the general belief is that it was the marked drop in temperature that sounded the death-knell for the Greenland venture.

The settlers' existence was largely forgotten over the next three hundred years. Following successful resettlement attempts in the eighteenth century, ruins of some of the early buildings were discovered, and subsequent archaeological digs have revealed a great deal. Examination of the human remains provides a grim picture of the malnutrition and disease which obviously overwhelmed the population over a period of years.

The demise of the Greenland colony remains the only known case of a well-developed and technologically advanced European settlement being wiped out by the weather, and is thus of special interest to modern-day climatologists.

Incas presenting offerings to their Sun God, circa 1550.

The magnificent stonemasonry skill of the Incas is visible in this view of a street in Cuzco, Peru.

The Demise of the Inca

The fabulous Inca civilisation flowered across large areas of South America from around 1250 to 1550, proving that Europe was not the only crucible of knowledge and learning during this era.

The Inca were a tribe or group of tribes from the area of what is now Cuzco in Peru. In early medieval times they began to expand into large areas of modern Ecuador, Peru, Bolivia and Chile, and parts of Colombia and Argentina. The Inca were benevolent conquerors and used the local leaders of the areas they took over as part of their ruling regime. Those who cooperated were treated very well, and in effect became part of the Inca 'family', although the Inca retained ultimate control. At the height of its power the Incan empire had a population of around one million people.

Inca society was strictly ordered and centralised. At the top was the head man or 'Inca', considered a direct descendant of the Sun God. His immediate family formed a ruling class that was above tribal heads, clan leaders and ultimately the common people, but all were bound together through a 'one for all, all for one' philosophy. Conquered peoples were required to pay a tribute tax to the ruling class, the revenue being used for widespread construction of roads and hillside terraces for farming.

The Inca were astonishingly technically advanced for the time. They were active in medicine (including surgery) and astronomy; they were industrious and effective farmers, growing such crops as potatoes and corn; and they were also accomplished engineers. Some incredible construction feats were achieved in extremely mountainous and rugged terrain, including many kilometres of roads, aqueducts and bridges. Their stonemasonry is still admired today—vast stone blocks cut so precisely that no mortar was required. Fine examples of this construction remain today in Cuzco, formerly the central city of the Incan empire.

> The Inca…were active in medicine…and astronomy; they were industrious and effective farmers, growing such crops as potatoes and corn; and they were also accomplished engineers.

In 1521 the Spanish conquistadors, led by Cortes, invaded the Inca lands. A second wave of conquistadors under Pizarro followed ten years later. The Spanish were searching for gold, conquest and new territories to settle and they thought the Incas would be an easy target.

The Incan ruler Atahualapa was executed by Pizarro and the Spaniards effectively took control of the empire. Spanish rule, combined with the smallpox that the Spaniards had brought with them, ultimately led to the demise of the Incan civilisation, with many of the once-great cities and towns falling into disrepair and shrinking to a fraction of their former size and significance.

In 1911, Professor Hiram Bingham of Yale was searching for the lost Inca city of Vilcabamba, high in the Peruvian Andes. On coming across the ruins of an amazing settlement perched high in a saddle between two mountain peaks, he thought he had found it. But he had stumbled on the fabled city of Machu Picchu, its whereabouts forgotten for around four hundred years. This city, carefully sculpted to fit into the surrounding steep terrain, had been one of the jewels of the Incan empire, and survived largely intact because the Spanish never found it. It is a much admired tourist destination today and possibly one of the most photographed locations in South America.

Many of the indigenous peoples of Peru are believed to be direct descendants of the Inca, a source of genuine local pride.

Henry VIII is Excommunicated

Succeeding to the throne of England in 1509, King Henry VIII was determined from the outset to have a son to succeed him, and became increasingly irritated with his queen, Catherine of Aragon, when she 'failed' to provide him with one.

At the time Henry's stocks with the Roman Catholic Church were high, for he had previously attacked the early Protestant reformer Martin Luther King in print and was noted as an ardent supporter of the Church. The Pope gave Henry the title 'Defender of the Faith' in 1521.

As was the custom of the times for a king, Henry had several mistresses, one of whom bore him a son, but since the child was illegitimate he could never become king. Henry became infatuated with Catherine's beautiful maid of honour, Anne Boleyn, and determined to marry her in the belief that she would provide him with a son. To do this he had to divorce Catherine, a procedure not normally permitted by the Church, and personally appealed his case to Rome. Apparently he felt confident of success because of his staunch defence of the Church some years before, perhaps feeling that he was owed a favour.

After several years of complex and fruitless wrangling with Pope Clement VII, Henry became increasingly angry, and began a process of lessening the Church's power in the government of England by appointing laymen into important positions such as those of Lord Chancellor and Lord Privy Seal, previously the domain of churchmen.

In 1533, after a series of events that further widened the rift with Rome, the Pope formally excommunicated Henry, producing an immediate and major religious upheaval in Britain. During 1534 the English parliament, largely under Henry's influence, passed several Acts that dramatically reduced the power of the Church in Britain, and placed the authority of the king above the pope in all matters of state. To refuse to acknowledge this was deemed treasonous, and immediately punishable by death.

The parliament validated the marriage between Henry and Anne Boleyn, and at the same time declared that Lady Mary, Catherine's daughter and only living child by Henry, was illegitimate. At this injustice, considerable unease arose across England, particularly among the Catholic clergy. Any opposition was soon to be met with brutal repression, including torture and execution. Henry also set about appropriating the assets of many of England's monasteries, setting up an Act of Parliament in 1536 specifically for this purpose.

Changes to the law also made it possible for Henry to divorce whenever he wished, and to have access to all Church moneys in England—both highly desirable outcomes from his point of view. Henry married again four times, with only one son resulting from all his unions (the future King Edward VI).

The Church of England, whose origins dated back to Anglo-Saxon times, had been unified with Rome for over a thousand years. Following Henry's actions the break between England and Rome was virtually complete—although there was a brief reunion in 1533 under Queen Mary I. The Church of England began moving away from Rome, to later become part of the Reformation that affected much of western Europe over the next hundred years. Henry's son, Edward, was to assist in this progression when he supervised the revision of much of the Roman Catholic liturgy along emerging Protestant lines, and published Thomas Cranmer's *Book of Common Prayer* in 1549, authorised by parliamentary decree.

Portrait of King Henry VIII, circa 1530.

The Great Fire rages through the streets of London, 1666.

The Great Fire of London

Much of the London that existed up until 1666 had been built in medieval times, some of it after a huge fire had destroyed large tracts of the city in 1212. The city was an undisciplined sprawl of tightly packed wooden housing and retail establishments of all kinds, much of it of two-storeyed construction.

Hay for horse feed lay about in quantity, and large heaps of firewood were stored in most yards to feed the thousands of open fires lit nightly to warm the population, particularly during the frigid winter months. But most significantly, many roofs were thatched with straw, and sealed with tar and pitch, making for a highly inflammable mix.

Firefighting had become completely disorganised following the departure of the Romans in 415, and nearly six hundred years later depended largely on individual households making their own arrangements with buckets and shovels. In the event of a big fire such defences were virtually useless.

By 1666 over four hundred and fifty years had passed since the last major conflagration. The real miracle was that it took so long for the inevitable to occur. On the night of 2 September 1666, a fire began in a baker's shop in Pudding Lane, gradually taking hold while the householders slept soundly upstairs. They finally awoke in the early hours to find the building ablaze, and a strong easterly wind blowing sparks and burning debris onto nearby buildings.

In a very short time a devastating fire took hold, raging towards the wharf areas along the Thames. These were lined with large warehouses crammed with flammable materials such as spirits, wine, brandy, tallow and oil. About seven hours after the fire began the flames were racing at great speed across the helpless city; all attempts to extinguish or even impede the blaze proved utterly futile.

The businessman Samuel Pepys was an eyewitness to the disaster and wrote in his famous diary:

So I rode down to the waterside ... and there saw a lamentable fire ... Everybody endeavouring to remove their goods, and flinging into the river or bringing them into lighters that lay off; poor people staying in their houses as long as till the very fire touched them, and then running into boats, or clambering from one pair of stairs by the waterside to another.

Diary 1660–1669

Desperate attempts to create firebreaks by demolishing buildings and even blowing them up with gunpowder were made—to little avail. The fire raged for another three days before eventually dying out near Whitehall.

The extent of the damage was staggering: an estimated 80 per cent of the city of London had been destroyed.

Incredibly, only six people were reported killed—but it's likely that the actual death toll was far greater.

Ironically, some good also came out of the fire: a large percentage of London's rats perished in the blaze and the incidence of outbreaks of bubonic plague fell sharply soon after.

London was never to be the same again. Diverse social changes triggered by the disaster included a move away from wooden construction, the banning of thatch as a roofing material, to be replaced by tile or slate, the development of household insurance schemes and the establishment of teams of professional fire-fighters. The Great Fire remains one of the defining events in the history of London, a dividing line separating medieval times from the modern era.

Arthur Miller used the Salem witch hunts in his play The Crucible *to attack McCarthyism.*

The trial of one of the men accused of witchcraft, George Jacobs.

The Salem Witch Hunts

During the period when much of Europe was reeling under the murderous regime of the Inquisition, the Puritans of colonial New England in America had their own experience of 'dancing with the Devil'.

The Puritans were honest, upright, God-fearing people who were deeply religious in their everyday affairs. But they were also superstitious: they believed in the Devil and in black magic, and were fearful of witches and witchcraft. Witchcraft was believed to be the selling of one's soul to the Devil in exchange for supernatural powers; this was seen as such a serious threat to the community that it was punishable by death.

In 1692, in the village of Salem in Massachusetts, the daughter and the niece of a local clergyman, the Reverend Samuel Parris, began convulsing and having hysterical fits. A doctor called in to investigate could find nothing physically wrong with the girls, and pronounced that their condition was likely the result of witchcraft.

The two girls then denounced Tituba (a South American Indian woman who was a slave attached to the Parris household), together with two other local women, Sarah Good and Sarah Osborn, as witches who had cast a spell on them. While an accusation of this type today would be considered laughable, in Salem during 1692 it was a very serious matter indeed.

All three women were brought before two local magistrates and closely questioned. The line of interrogation virtually assumed that they were guilty of witchcraft, an offence that carried the death penalty. In the best traditions of the Inquisition in Europe, the only way to avoid death was to admit guilt, and receive a gaol sentence instead. Under the pressure of the intense interrogations, Tituba eventually gave way and 'admitted' she had made a pact with the Devil and become a witch, and had in fact flown through the night sky on a broomstick. She also pointed an accusing finger at Sarah Good and Sarah Osborn.

These developments threw the people of Salem into a state of hysteria, and over the next few months the residents feverishly searched for other witches within their ranks. Hearsay or gossip was enough to bring a person before the courts, and soon the ranks of female accused were joined by several men, also charged with having become witches. Eventually some 150 local men and women were waiting in prison for their trials to begin.

Those who refused to admit their 'crimes' were hanged, and the remainder thrown into prison. One man was pressed to death under large stones when he refused to recant. The situation was rapidly spiralling out of control. Perhaps realising this, Governor William Phipps disbanded the 'witchcraft' courts in October 1692, released the prisoners and pardoned those who were marked for execution. The ghastly charade was over, but twenty men and women, all innocent citizens, had been executed and many more unjustly imprisoned as a result of the superstitious hysteria.

As the years went by it became increasingly obvious that a terrible miscarriage of justice had been committed. Apologies and financial compensation were offered to the families of the victims. For many, of course, this was too late.

In 1952, the famous playwright Arthur Miller wrote *The Crucible* which, although based on the Salem witch hunts, was an indirect attack on McCarthyism—the attempt to identify and destroy the careers of communist sympathisers in America. Miller believed that McCarthy's activities were a modern day form of the 'witch hunt' that had plagued New England some two hundred and sixty years earlier.

The Greatest Storm in Europe

Before the beginning of organised meteorological services around the world in the nineteenth century, there were many occasions when wild weather produced widespread loss of life. This was particularly true on the oceans, where ships' captains had to put to sea with little or no knowledge of the weather that lay ahead.

One of the very worst of these unforeseen occurrences was the infamous tempest of 26–27 November 1703, when gale-force winds blasted across England and Europe, producing death and destruction on a major scale. Because little official meteorological information was being recorded at that time, it is likely that details of the storm would have been forgotten but for the publication of a book containing a particularly well-written and detailed account of the incident by a budding young author who would later become world famous. The book, released in the following year, was entitled simply *The Storm*. It was the first book written by Daniel Defoe, later renowned as the author of the classic *Robinson Crusoe*.

Meteorologists subsequently reconstructing the event believe that on the night of 26 November 1703, an intense low-pressure cell located to the north-east of Scotland was directing gale-force winds from the south-west across Ireland, Wales and southern England. This is not an uncommon situation, but in this case the weather was made significantly worse by what meteorologists call a 'secondary low', a smaller scale vortex embedded in the circulation of the main low-pressure cell. A secondary low may be only around 160 kilometres across—the main circulation could be ten times larger—but this small, intense vortex can greatly magnify the local winds, and produce a well-defined damage trail across the ground.

> The sails of windmills rotated so fast that the internal gears caught fire from the tremendous frictional heat generated, and some four hundred were destroyed by fire.

In this case it is believed that a secondary low tore across Wales at around 3 am on 26 November, reaching London at about 6 am, then curving north-east across the North Sea to reach Copenhagen in Denmark later in the morning. While no accurate wind measurements were made, analysis of the damage reports indicates that average winds were probably well in excess of 160 kilometres per hour, cutting a wide trail of destruction across southern England and western Europe. London, which only thirty-seven years earlier had been devastated by the Great Fire, sustained tremendous damage. Thousands of roofs were stripped, many houses completely blown down, and numerous church spires destroyed.

The sails of windmills rotated so fast that the internal gears caught fire from the tremendous frictional heat generated, and some four hundred were destroyed by fire. Many thousands of trees were blown down, killing huge numbers of sheep and cattle. But by far the worst events took place at sea, where it is estimated that around a hundred large ships were sunk, and up to eight thousand sailors drowned.

Analysing weather events of the past is always difficult, particularly where no accurate records were taken, but many meteorologists believe that the 1703 storm was one of the most extreme weather events to affect the area for at least the last five hundred years, if not in recorded history.

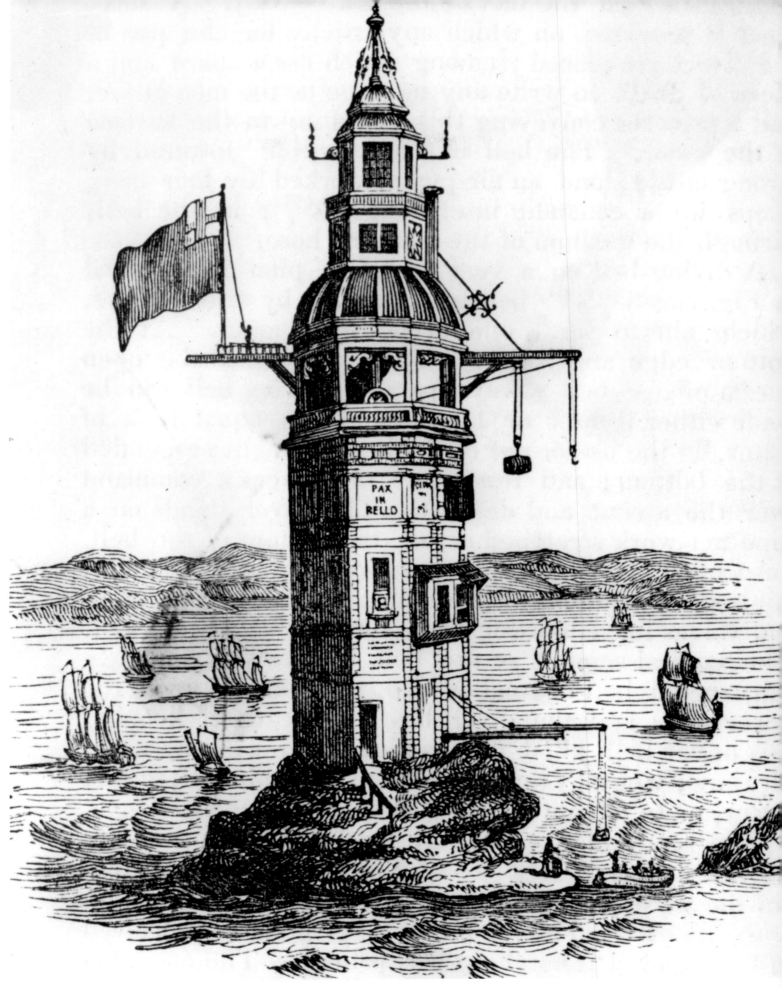

Winstanley Tower, an early lighthouse erected on the Eddystone Rocks, was destroyed by the storm in 1703.

The death of Admiral Nelson during the battle.

The naval flags depicting Nelson's famous signal 'England expects that every man will do his duty'.

The Battle of Trafalgar

Just before noon on 21 October 1805, as the two fleets were preparing for the conflict, Nelson sent out what was to become one of the most famous naval signals of history: 'England expects that every man will do his duty'.

Horatio Nelson was born in 1758 and joined the British Navy as a boy. Showing leadership qualities right from the outset, he became a ship's captain at only twenty years of age, and saw action at sea as a commander soon after. He was known for his bold and daring manoeuvres, but his fearlessness was tempered by a deep concern and compassion for the men under his command, who universally held him in high regard. His great personal bravery often placed him in considerable danger, and he lost the sight of his right eye, and later lost his right arm, in naval battles.

Nelson was not above disobeying the orders of superiors if he thought he could do better; at the Battle of Copenhagen in 1801 he famously ignored orders to cease action by putting a telescope to his blind eye and later claiming he had not seen the signal ordering a retreat.

His dash, bravery and naval skills made him a national hero in England, while the fact that he was married but also conducting a very public affair with his mistress, Lady Hamilton, did nothing to decrease his tremendous public appeal.

Britain's global naval superiority was well established during the eighteenth century, firmly underpinning the vital mercantile trade upon which the nation so heavily depended. In the early nineteenth century the greatest ever threat to this superiority came from France. Napoleon was planning to invade southern England, but had to smash the Royal Navy to do so. To this end, he intended to assemble a combined French and Spanish fleet to provide the necessary cannon power.

The Royal Navy sent out their best leader to command the vital upcoming battle—Horatio Nelson, recently promoted to admiral. History reveals he was the perfect choice. After considerable manoeuvring, the British fleet, consisting of 27 fighting ships, squared off against the Franco-Spanish fleet, numbering 33 ships, off the coast of Cape Trafalgar, south-west Spain. The British were heavily outnumbered in personnel and firepower, with 17 000 men and 2148 guns facing around 30 000 French and Spanish seamen with 2568 guns.

Just before noon on 21 October 1805, as the two fleets were preparing for the conflict, Nelson sent out what was to become one of the most famous naval signals of history: 'England expects that every man will do his duty'. He then ordered the Royal Navy to attack.

Despite the considerable odds against him, Nelson's bold and unorthodox tactics proved more than a match for the larger force, and after some three hours of savage and lethal fighting the French and Spanish surrendered. But a terrible calamity had occurred during the battle—a French sniper had shot and mortally wounded Admiral Nelson as he stood on the deck of his flagship *Victory*, and he died soon afterwards.

News of the great battle reached England, where there was unbounded joy on learning of the defeat of the enemy, but national grief upon hearing of the death of Nelson. His body, carried home on the *Victory*, reached England in December and lay in state at the Greenwich Hospital, where many thousands of mourners filed past.

On 8 January 1806, amid unprecedented scenes, London virtually came to a halt as a massive state funeral honoured Nelson's memory, and his remains were taken up the Thames River by barge to Westminster. His coffin was interred at St Paul's Cathedral the next day, sealing his reputation as the most famous and honoured of all admirals in the history of the Royal Navy.

The Eruption of Mount Tambora

Mount Tambora is an active volcano situated on the Indonesian island of Sumbawa. It was the scene of one of the greatest volcanic blasts known in human existence, producing an immediate and terrible death toll in the local area and disturbing the atmosphere to such an extent that its effects were felt around the world for the next two years or so.

The phenomenal eruption occurred over the five-day period of 10–16 April 1815. A series of violent explosions threw many millions of tonnes of rock and ash high into the atmosphere. The noise from these explosions was so loud that it was heard in parts of Borneo, over 800 kilometres away. Around 10 000 people died almost immediately in the near vicinity, killed by debris, superheated gases and lava flows; an estimated 80 000 later perished from around Indonesia as a result of ash accumulating in their lungs, and from famine caused by crop failures due to changed weather conditions.

The vast amount of powder-fine volcanic ash ejected high into the atmosphere gradually extended around the Earth and is thought to have produced the 'Year Without a Summer' in faraway Europe and North America in 1816. Climate scientists believe that the sulphurous ash combined with atmospheric water vapour to form a 'shield' high in the atmosphere that reflected a significant amount of incoming solar energy back into space, resulting in abnormally cool weather over large areas.

Particularly hard hit were northern Europe and north-eastern America, where the amazingly cold summer resulted in widespread crop failures, starvation and even civil unrest. Heavy frosts occurred across parts of north-eastern

> Heavy frosts occurred across parts of north-eastern America in late spring and even early summer, and unprecedented heavy snow fell in June, resulting in a large death toll.

America in late spring and even early summer, and unprecedented heavy snow fell in June, resulting in a large death toll. Some historians have related the associated crop failures to the subsequent attempts to push westward in search of more suitable farming conditions.

Europe was even more deeply affected, with England in 1816 seeing its coldest summer since the frigid years at the height of the Little Ice Age that devastated the area between 1350 and around 1800 and severe food shortages due to crop failures.

The unseasonably cold weather also produced starvation and food riots in France and Switzerland, where neither country could produce enough food to feed their populations. People were forced to eat 'sorrel, moss and cat flesh' to survive. The situation in Switzerland grew so serious that the government declared a national emergency in an attempt to stop the looting of warehouses. Other countries badly affected included Germany, the Netherlands and Ireland.

The impact of the eruption was felt even in the areas of art and literature. The ash cloud in the atmosphere produced spectacular red sunsets around the world, which are featured in some of the works of the English landscape artist J.M. Turner (1775–1851). It is also believed that the cold rainy summer across Switzerland

The frigid summer of 1816 led Mary Shelley to write Frankenstein *whilst holidaying in Switzerland.*

that year forced the holidaying Mary Shelley to spend much of her vacation indoors where, with nothing better to do, she penned her famous work *Frankenstein*.

Estimates of the total death toll from the eruption have varied widely, but if both direct and indirect mortalities are included, a worldwide figure of 200 000 seems possible. It was a chilling demonstration of the power of even one volcano to affect weather around the globe, with some experts predicting that it's only a matter of time before a similar event takes place.

The French cavalry in retreat during the Battle of Waterloo.

The Battle of Waterloo

The fight quickly descended into truly murderous carnage, with artillery barrages, cavalry charges and infantry attacks ebbing and flowing across the increasingly bloody battlefield.

After years of fighting across Europe, Emperor Napoleon of France was defeated in the Battle of the Nations at Liepzig in October 1813 and abdicated in April 1814. Banished to the island of Elba in the Mediterranean Sea, Napoleon soon plotted his escape, making his way back to Paris in late March 1815. He immediately began re-assembling his Grand Armée, and the allied forces of Holland, Belgium, Prussia and Britain that had defeated him previously were hurriedly reformed in response to the new threat.

Napoleon marched into Belgium, and in June 1815 advanced on the British and allied armies, commanded by the Duke of Wellington, whose forces took up position astride the main road to Brussels near a low ridge overlooking rolling agricultural land dotted with several farms. It was located in an area lying to the south of the nearby village of Waterloo.

Wellington's forces consisted of some 77 000 troops, including soldiers from Britain, Holland and Belgium; another allied force, the Prussians, numbering over 100 000 troops, was located only a few miles away. This combined force heavily outnumbered Napoleon's 72 000 soldiers, some of them veterans of the Grand Armée of previous years. Both sides possessed substantial forces of infantry, cavalry and artillery.

On the surface, these figures pointed to overwhelming military superiority for Wellington, but they masked the true situation. His army was a mixture of nationalities, and internal communications were difficult because of language problems. Many of his troops were inexperienced in battle, with varying motivation and taste for conflict. Wellington was obliged to mix his forces, with dependable troops interspersed with the 'marginals' to prevent mass desertions. He later referred to the forces under his control as 'an infamous army'.

In addition, the large force of Prussians, although only some 13 kilometres from Wellington's position, was not immediately available for battle (13 kilometres was a long way in 1815).

In contrast, Napoleon's army was homogeneous, more experienced and motivated and, with battle-hardened commanders, capable of executing fast, integrated military manoeuvres.

The stage was set for one of the great conflicts of the nineteenth century, which took place on 18 June 1815, and was to become known as the Battle of Waterloo.

On the night of 17 June, a solid downpour drenched both sides and soaked the countryside between them. The French were forced to delay their planned dawn bombardment as the ground was too soft for the manoeuvring of their field guns. They began their assault at 11 am—a late start by military standards.

The fight quickly descended into truly murderous carnage, with artillery barrages, cavalry charges and infantry attacks ebbing and flowing across the increasingly bloody battlefield. The actual area of conflict was small, around 10 by 4 kilometres, leading to a high concentration of forces, and a continuous terrific noise throughout the day.

The outcome remained in the balance until well into the afternoon, when the Prussians finally arrived, having been slowed in their advance by the boggy conditions. With this injection of large numbers of fresh troops, the French were simply overwhelmed, and eventually retreated from the battlefield.

The British and allied forces had won a great victory, but the price was high—it was later estimated that one in four soldiers had died on the battlefield that day, not to mention the large numbers of wounded, often permanently incapacitated men who returned home to a difficult existence.

The Irish Potato Famine

The late fifteenth and early sixteenth centuries were hard times for Ireland, involving extended periods of warfare against England and internal conflicts between local power groups. The incessant fighting was disastrous for agricultural production—farming land, mostly occupied by tenant farmers, was periodically overrun by soldiers and ruined.

Because of unjust tenancy laws, it was impossible for a tenant farmer ever to have a large area of land under cultivation. Even more difficult, there was no known crop that was hardy enough, could provide sufficient nourishment and could be grown in large enough quantity from a small allotment to service the average-sized family. Starvation was common among peasant farmers and their offspring in those years.

However, about 1600 the potato arrived in Ireland—some say from a wrecked ship of the Spanish Armada—and this was to dramatically change farming practices right across the country. The potato fulfilled all of Ireland's food needs—it was hardy and highly nutritious and sufficient could be grown from a small plot to feed a family. Perhaps most importantly, in the event of the farm being trampled over by invaders, potatoes could be recovered later from beneath the soil and readily grown again. By the 1800s the humble potato came to be a major food source across the country, and the primary source of sustenance for several million people.

It was against this background that total disaster struck in the middle of the century. An infectious fungal disease, known at the time as the potato blight (and later identified as *Phytophthora infestans*), almost totally ruined the potato crop of 1845. Similar crop disasters in 1846 and 1848 left millions of people teetering on the brink of starvation. Weakened by hunger, many succumbed to diseases such as cholera and typhus, with large numbers actually starving to death over the period 1845–55.

England offered assistance, but it was meagre and unsatisfactory. Some of the more conservative elements of the English government ignored the human dimension and considered that it would be improper to 'interfere with the market' by handing out free food. Later some relief was provided in the form of soup kitchens and 'workhouses' but such attempts were entirely overwhelmed by the immense scale of the problem.

In desperation, many Irish fled their country and travelled to England, America and Canada in ships that were so overcrowded and unsanitary that many more died; these vessels became known as the 'Coffin Ships'. Over a million people left Ireland in what turned out to be one of the great mass migrations in history, forever changing the population mix of both the Old and the New World.

There are widely differing estimates of how many people died in the famine, from both starvation and disease, but figures of around one million are common. Combined with the mass emigration, the population of Ireland may have been reduced by as much as 25 per cent in a few short years.

The perceived lack of support from England created an extended period of bitterness, and many Irish believe to this day that the English deliberately ignored their plight for selfish economic reasons.

Potato blight remains a threat to potato crops even in modern times, even though fungicides have been partially successful in controlling its spread.

A starving mother and children scour the ground for potatoes at the height of the famine.

President Lincoln (centre) visits the Union troops at Antietam, Maryland in 1862.

The American Civil War

The battle lines between forces of the Union and the Confederates were now drawn; it was only a matter of time before conflict began, eventually triggered when President Abraham Lincoln sent Union troops to recapture some federal forts occupied by the Confederates.

During the 1850s, the United States had become increasingly polarised ideologically and economically. Different systems of wages and labour had evolved: in the north, there was a developing wages-based industrial and agricultural economy; slavery was strictly forbidden. The south, however, depended on large plantations, particularly cotton—then, as now, a highly successful cash crop. In sharp contrast to the situation in the north, the labour force that serviced this plantation economy was provided largely by black slaves. The increasingly sharp ideological and economic division between north and south was one of the major causes of the conflict to follow.

Events escalated in February 1861, when seven southern states seceded from the American Union and declared themselves the Confederate States of America. The battle lines between forces of the Union and the Confederates were now drawn; it was only a matter of time before conflict began, eventually triggered when President Abraham Lincoln sent Union troops to recapture some federal forts occupied by the Confederates.

In July 1861, in the First Battle of Bull Run, Union forces attacked the Confederates in Virginia. This was the first major battle of the unfolding American Civil War. A series of bloody conflicts followed. The fortunes of the war ebbed and flowed over the next four years, producing a terrible and ever-mounting death toll. The generals who directed the battles became household names around the world, Robert E. Lee of the Confederates and Ulysses S. Grant of the Union being perhaps the two best known.

In 1862, near Sharpsburg in Maryland, Lee's troops were defeated in the Battle of Antietam: this turned out to be the day on which the greatest number of Americans were ever killed in battle in a 24-hour period occurred—about 4800. This gruesome record still stands, not exceeded even by the utter carnage of the two World Wars.

Early in 1864, Union forces began to get the upper hand. Now in command of the entire northern army, General Grant adopted a 'scorched-earth policy'—which involved the destruction of crops, transport and communications in an effort to cripple the Confederacy economically and socially as well as militarily—and his troops made several simultaneous attacks on the south. The Union's far superior naval forces were also able to blockade and isolate the major Confederate ports, including New Orleans and Charleston, thus depriving the Confederate land forces of food supplies, arms and ammunition.

The Confederates gradually weakened and were forced to retreat; on 9 April 1865 the inevitable happened and Lee surrendered to Grant at the Appomattox Court House. The great and terrible American Civil War was over.

This war remains the bloodiest conflict in America's history. Three million soldiers fought for over four years in what remains the only war actually waged on American soil and in which, most tragically, over 600 000 people were killed.

The immediate effect of the war was to officially end slavery in America, but it also resulted in a significant shift in political power towards the northern states. This, together with the effects of Grant's brutal scorched-earth policy, resulted in decades of anti-northern bitterness in the south, which only gradually began to wear off well into the twentieth century. Even today pockets of resentment still exist.

Booth arrived … armed with a hunting knife and a 44-calibre derringer pistol, both hidden in his clothing.

Booth creeps up behind Lincoln in the private box above the stage.

Booth escapes the theatre after leaping onto the stage from Lincoln's box.

The Assassination of Abraham Lincoln

Probably the greatest casualty of the American Civil War was the man who played a primary role in starting it—Abraham Lincoln, the sixteenth President of the United States. While revered by most in the north as the victor of the war and the abolisher of slavery, Confederate sympathisers bore him deep animosity and blamed him for all the problems experienced by the South, both during and after the war.

One of these was an eccentric actor, John Wilkes Booth. Well known in theatrical circles for his lead Shakespearean roles, Booth was a strong Southern sympathiser and a suspected spy for the South during the war. He was also believed to have smuggled medicines through Union blockades to the Confederate army. He deeply resented the outcome of the war and regarded Lincoln, above all else, as the architect of the South's troubles. His family had reportedly kept slaves when Booth was a boy, and Lincoln's giving slaves their freedom was said to have especially irritated him.

Well before the war ended, Booth and a group of five other like-minded Southerners had hatched a plan to kidnap Lincoln, take him to the Southern capital of Richmond, Virginia, and trade him for Confederate prisoners of war. This plan, due for execution on 17 March 1865, was thwarted by a change in Lincoln's schedule. Less than a month later, the South surrendered and Booth's plan evolved into something much more deadly.

Along with his conspirators, he planned an all-out assault on Lincoln and his senior political colleagues. On learning that Lincoln was due to attend Ford's Theatre in Washington on the evening of 14 April, Booth planned to shoot Lincoln during the performance, while his cohorts would assassinate the Vice-President and the Secretary of State in separate but simultaneous attacks elsewhere, all timed for 10.15 pm. Apart from revenge, Booth apparently considered that such an act would topple the government and bring on a Southern revival.

Booth arrived at the theatre soon after 10 pm, armed with a hunting knife and a 44-calibre derringer pistol, both hidden in his clothing. The derringer was only a very small single-shot weapon, but its heavy calibre made it deadly—especially at close range.

At 10.15, Booth quietly opened the door to the State box and came in behind Lincoln as the President watched the performance below. From very close range he fired into the back of Lincoln's head; the heavy calibre slug lodged deep in the President's brain.

Major Rathbone, who was accompanying Lincoln in the box, attempted to tackle the murderer but was repelled when Booth stabbed him in the arm. Booth then leapt spectacularly to the stage from the box, watched by the amazed audience, most of whom had no idea what had happened, and strode out the back door of the theatre to make his getaway on a waiting horse. President Lincoln lived for a short time but was pronounced dead early next morning.

The other parts of the plan failed completely. No attempt was made to kill the Vice-President, and the Secretary of State was stabbed but only wounded.

The conspirators fled for their lives with federal authorities in hot pursuit. Booth was shot and killed in a standoff twelve days later; the others were eventually captured, tried and hanged.

The Birth of the Mafia

The first official reference to 'the Mafia' appeared in 1865 in an official report from the Chief Prosecutor in Palermo, Sicily, in reference to criminal gangs proliferating in the area. Not long afterwards, the authorities recognised that the Mafia represented a different form of criminality to the usual.

Mafia is a Sicilian word literally meaning 'beautiful', but colloquially it also means 'proud, arrogant, fearless', words characterising the conduct of the Mafiosi, the members of the gangs. Another term by which the Mafia was known was Cosa Nostra, which roughly translates as 'this thing of ours'.

The Mafiosi were neither furtive nor secretive about their activities, seeing themselves as men of honour who supported traditional values. Instead of regarding them as criminals, the local people looked upon them with admiration: they were to some extent the protectors of the downtrodden of society, whose plight was largely ignored by the government of the day.

Another key difference between the Mafia and common criminality was its organisation. Mafia gangs, or clans, became highly structured groups with a well-defined chain of command directing operations, and a strict code of silence called omerta. To break this code, and inform the authorities about any Mafia activity, was immediately punishable by death.

The Mafia soon developed significant political power: members or sympathisers were entrenched in the government and the judiciary, and it gradually spread with increasing power onto the Italian mainland. Immigration brought the Mafia to the United States in the early twentieth century, where it rapidly took root in New York City and soon established a fearsome reputation across the country.

The Mafia evolved into a system of *famiglia* (families), each with a military-style structure headed by a *don* (godfather), and assisted by a *consigliere* (counsellor). The lower layers of command consisted of regimes each headed by a *caporegime* in command of numerous *soldati*, or 'soldiers'.

The main enterprises initially undertaken in the United States included robbery, extortion, loan sharking, illegal gambling and prostitution, but what added tremendous impetus to the American Mafia scene was the introduction of Prohibition in 1920. This created an enormous and highly lucrative black market for illicit liquor that the Mafia was only too willing to service. Bootlegging became one of the Mafia's most profitable ventures.

When Prohibition ended in 1933, the Mafia changed operational emphasis, with illicit drugs becoming increasingly important to their portfolio of crime.

During World War II, Benito Mussolini cracked down heavily on the Mafia in Italy, which as a result became strongly anti-fascist and a rather odd ally of the American government.

It was rumoured that during the war the American Mafia was given the unofficial job of keeping spies and insurgents away from the American docks, which according to some were extraordinarily trouble free during this period.

In 1969 the author Mario Puzo published his bestselling blockbuster novel *The Godfather*, a carefully researched account of the Corleones, a fictional New York Mafia family. The *Chicago Sun-Times* said frankly of the novel: 'This is the hard, chilling, incredible, brutal reality of the vice

> The Mafiosi were neither furtive nor secretive about their activities, seeing themselves as men of honour who supported traditional values.

Police photo of New York Mafia boss Vito Genovese, taken after his arrest in 1955.

that this nation tolerates'. The novel was followed by the highly successful movies *The Godfather I, II* and *III*, which further developed Puzo's theme.

The power of the Mafia in the United States has declined over the last thirty years or so, but it still maintains a significant presence.

Railway hunting trips were responsible for thousands of buffalo being shot.

Shooters fired from the roofs and windows of the train carriages.

Buffalo Slaughter

The American buffalo, more correctly bison, are believed to have reached the North American mainland from Asia during the last ice age. As the climate warmed again, herds moved southwards across the Great Plains area, where the vast grasslands proved an ideal habitat, and the species prospered.

The American buffalo is a magnificent animal that stands up to 1.8 metres high at the shoulder and is around 3.6 metres in length. Even though it may weigh upwards of 900 kilograms, it can run at speeds of 56 kilometres an hour for extended periods. It will also charge a human if provoked or cornered.

It is believed that, at their peak, buffalo numbers may have exceeded 50 million. For centuries they were a vital source of food and hides for Native Americans right across the Great Plains. Although they were constantly hunted, the numbers killed were never excessive, and the buffalo was respected as a noble neighbour of the prairie.

When Europeans came, they were astonished at the magnificent spectacle of apparently limitless herds of buffalo stretching as far as the eye could see. But it would soon be shown that the population was not unlimited; an unparalleled ecological disaster was averted only by the narrowest of margins.

Major problems began in the early 1870s, when professional hunters, making money from buffalo meat and hides, began shooting the animals on an ever-increasing scale. Large beasts grazing across open countryside with little or no cover were easy targets for a modern rifle.

Buffalo hides in particular were in demand; literally millions were taken from the prairie, stacked high on open wagons and transported to the nearest railhead for the next train east. Even more calamitous was the emergence of buffalo hunting as a 'sport'—tourists flocked to the plains to try their hand at killing a few beasts. Local railroads promoted buffalo hunting as an attraction for their service, with patrons invited to shoot at herds from the comfort of their carriage windows. This would sometimes continue until there was no ammunition left or until the rifles became too hot to hold.

If the hunter was interested only in the hide, the skinned carcass would be left to rot on the prairie where it fell. Observers reported the rolling countryside dotted with the pale mounds of hundreds of skinned buffalo. Sporting shooters didn't even bother to take the hide.

> Local railroads promoted buffalo hunting as an attraction for their service, with patrons invited to shoot at herds from the comfort of their carriage windows.

Perhaps the worst justification for this mass slaughter came from some government officials, who reasoned that eliminating the herds would force the Native Americans into submission by starvation and drive them onto the reservations so that their lands could be taken easily. This policy was enthusiastically adopted, and further wholesale killing was conducted by the army. For a time it seemed that nothing could save the buffalo from total extinction.

When the killings had finally run their course, only a few hundred animals remained from the mighty herds of millions that had roamed the plains only a short time before. Since then the buffalo's numbers have gradually increased under strict protection in several national parks, notably Yellowstone in Wyoming.

Paintings of the battle reveal a scene of confusion and terror.

Custer is seen in this painting as the heroic central figure.

Custer's Last Stand: the Battle of the Little Bighorn

George Armstrong Custer's military career began inauspiciously at West Point Military Academy, where he just scraped through, finishing last in his class in June 1861.

Almost immediately, he found himself in action during the American Civil War, where he forged a reputation as an impetuous but brave cavalryman. He fought with great gallantry and distinction on several occasions and became well known to both his superiors and the general public. After the war, in 1866, he was promoted to lieutenant colonel, and later led the 7th Cavalry on several campaigns during the 'Indian Wars'.

In June 1876 Custer was pushing deep into the plains of Montana, accompanied by two other generals, Gibbon and Crook, in search of Indian villages. The lead-up to this was a government ultimatum to the Sioux and Cheyenne tribes of the area, ordering them to return to a reservation by the last day of January 1876—an edict which they chose to ignore. The government then ordered the mounting of a full military campaign to compel the tribes to obey, using whatever force was deemed necessary.

Well aware of the approaching threat, the Sioux and Cheyenne banded together in a vast village of some eight to ten thousand people in the valley of the Little Bighorn River, headed by the great Sioux leader Sitting Bull. Indian scouts attached to Custer's force finally found them there on 25 June 1876.

Custer headed a detachment of the 7th Cavalry, consisting of some 647 mounted troops armed with modern rifles and equipped with all the standard-issue gear of the day. It was generally believed that a force of this type would have no problems in dealing with any sort of Indian threat, and Custer did not have a high opinion of his opposition.

> They found themselves rapidly surrounded and outnumbered by hundreds of mounted warriors, to be gradually worn down and picked off by the circling braves.

But modern analysis has shown that far from being battlefield cowards, the mounted Plains Indians were among the finest light cavalry in the history of warfare. A typical Sioux or Cheyenne warrior was fit and brave and could ride bareback across broken ground at full gallop, accurately firing arrows at the same time. It would be convincingly demonstrated that these sorts of skills more than compensated for any formal lack of knowledge of military tactics.

Forgetting one of the oldest and most basic military axioms—never underestimate your enemy—Custer and his force attacked the village, expecting the Sioux and Cheyenne to flee, or at the very worst to put up some form of light resistance only.

Instead, they found themselves rapidly surrounded and outnumbered by hundreds of mounted warriors, to be gradually worn down and picked off by the circling braves. At the end of the day, amid a rapidly rising squall of dust kicked up by hundreds of horses, some 263 soldiers, including Custer himself, were dead in what was one of the US army's greatest battlefield defeats. The Sioux and Cheyenne broke camp and disbanded into the wilderness, leaving Custer's men lying where they fell on the prairie grass.

When the news reached Washington, it was met with consternation and disbelief. But instead of being portrayed as a military incompetent, Custer was elevated to the status of folk hero, shown in innumerable paintings and sketches standing heroically on a hillside surrounded by hordes of screaming savages. 'Custer's Last Stand' became an iconic image of the American West.

Krakatoa

On 27 August 1883 the volcano Mount Krakatoa, on the Indonesian island of Rakata, exploded with phenomenal violence. This was only some sixty-eight years after the eruption of another Indonesian volcano, Mount Tambora, on the nearby island of Sumbawa, which produced a gigantic ash cloud that circled Earth.

Krakatoa, too, produced vast quantities of ash that reached the highest levels of the atmosphere. However, the main feature of this eruption was the noise, which is believed to have been the loudest sound ever heard in recorded human history.

A sonic shock-wave tore around the world, and the sound of the eruption was heard as rolling thunder as far away as Perth in Western Australia, and Rodriguez Island near Mauritius—both over 3200 kilometres distant. Barographs (instruments that measure atmospheric pressure) around the world recorded pressure fluctuations from the blast.

The explosion itself destroyed many villages in the vicinity of the volcano, but the worst effect was a series of tsunamis: waves in excess of 30 metres in height bore down on the coastlines of nearby islands, carrying away all before them.

Several vessels sailing in the Sunda Straits recorded the onset of these giant waves. The passengers and crew of one ship, the *Gouverneur-Generaal Loudon*, witnessed the destruction of the coastal town of Telok Betong on the island of Sumatra:

> Suddenly we saw a gigantic wave of prodigious height advancing toward the seashore with considerable speed ... The wave continued on its journey toward land, and the benumbed crew watched as the sea in a single sweeping motion consumed the town. There, where an instant before had lain the town of Telok Betong, nothing remained but the open sea.

Eyewitness account of a passenger on the *Gouverneur-Generaal Loudon*

Over 30 000 people died in the disaster, mostly as a result of tsunami activity, and some 150 coastal villages were obliterated. Tidal gauges around the globe recorded ocean level disturbances from the tsunamis.

Other extraordinary effects were produced by the mighty blast. The eruption produced phenomenal amounts of pumice (a porous volcanic rock that floats on water), vast rafts of which floated about the sea according to the surface currents, some of it crossing the Indian Ocean in about a year. This phenomenon greatly interested scientists of the day, as it seemed to raise the possibility that plant life and even small animal organisms could travel between continents on such rafts.

Because of the blanket of fine volcanic dust circling Earth, extraordinarily vivid red sunsets were reported from around the world for the next two to three years; it is estimated that there was a general cooling of global temperatures over the next five years due to the reflective effect of this mantle.

This cooling effect was smaller than that produced by the Tambora eruption of 1815, and thus some climate scientists believe that less atmospheric debris was involved.

Forty-four years later, in early 1927, local fishermen reported columns of steam venting from the surface of the ocean in the area of the great eruption. The next year, the world's vulcanologists were fascinated by the reports of the birth of a new volcanic island—Anak Krakatoa ('son of Krakatoa')—as an ashy landmass slowly rose above the waves.

The main feature of this eruption was the noise, which is believed to have been the loudest sound ever heard in recorded human history.

A painting of the eruption showing the massive ash cloud.

Bucks Row, East London, where one of the victims was found.

Jack the Ripper

In the nineteenth century, London was one of the world's largest cities, with a sprawling metropolis expanding to accommodate a rapidly increasing population. By 1830 around two million people lived in the city, a doubling of the population in only thirty years.

Teeming slums sprawled across many areas, particularly in what was known as the 'East End'. Health problems were a major issue; polluted drinking water and an inadequate sewerage system contributed to periodic outbreaks of typhoid and cholera. Dickensian poverty was rampant in the slums, where survival was a constant battle, and a hand-to-mouth existence the only possible lifestyle for many. Some women were forced into casual prostitution just to survive and provide a few extra pennies for their families.

At night the streets around the East End were dangerous, with frequent muggings and assaults overstretching the resources of the Metropolitan Police Force and the newly formed Criminal Investigations Department—later known as Scotland Yard. Night constables on foot patrolled the cold, fog-enshrouded streets dimly lit by the hissing gaslights that had been progressively installed across the city during the early 1800s. It was in these mean streets, around the Whitechapel area in the East End, that a series of murders took place that horrified the police, the general public and even the locals, who were in general thoroughly accustomed to crime and violence.

Between August and November 1888, five women were brutally murdered in the area and severely mutilated after death. All were prostitutes; four of the five were in their forties, the other only twenty-five years old.

It was the nature of the mutilations that both horrified the population and titillated the press. The victims had been either strangled or stabbed to death. Then all had their throats slashed with a sharp knife, and some had body parts removed, including a heart, uterus and kidney. Because of the nature of these 'operations', many believed that the perpetrator had to have knowledge of anatomy, and therefore could be a butcher, or even a doctor. The murderer was dubbed 'Jack the Ripper' as police began one of the biggest manhunts in British history. Serial killers were unusual in those days, and the emerging British tabloid press produced vast amounts of sensational copy that was devoured by a horrified yet fascinated public.

Police and newspapers were deluged with letters claiming to have information about the killer, with a few correspondents even claiming to be the murderer—most of these 'confessional' letters were considered hoaxes. Despite the scale and thoroughness of the investigation, no arrest was ever made.

An interesting social consequence was the publicity given to the plight of the East End poor. Many well-heeled citizens of London were shocked to find that middle-aged women were forced into prostitution just to feed their families. This laid at least some of the basis for the social reform that was to gather momentum in the early twentieth century.

The Jack the Ripper murders became a firm part of urban folklore, both in Britain and overseas. Hundreds of investigations were undertaken over the next century by professionals, amateurs and even psychics in attempts to solve the mystery, with several investigators later claiming to have 'solved' the crime. Perhaps no other criminal case has spawned so many conspiracy theories, but no universally accepted explanation has ever surfaced.

> All had their throats slashed with a sharp knife, and some had body parts removed, including a heart, uterus and kidney.

A tree trunk piercing the second floor of a house reveals the power of the floodwaters.

Johnstown Dam Collapse

On Memorial Day, 30 May 1889, the city of Johnstown, situated in Pennsylvania's Conemaugh Valley, celebrated its history with a large, patriotic street march that attracted big crowds along its route. Johnstown had grown from humble beginnings to a large industrial settlement of over 20 000 people. This was thanks mainly to the Cambria Iron Company, an extensive industrial enterprise that supplied employment to a significant part of the local population.

Johnstown was built at the junction of two small rivers, the Little Conemaugh River and Stony Creek, their confluence forming the main Conemaugh River. The Little Conemaugh began its life in the mountains above a large reservoir, the South Fork Dam. The earth and rubble dam had been constructed in the 1830s by the state of Pennsylvania. The South Fork Dam was later abandoned by the state and bought out by a private consortium that, possibly without the benefit of engineering advice, raised the dam wall and stocked the artificial mountain lake with fish.

Fishing was only one of the attractions of the lakeside South Fork Fishing and Hunting Club, a holiday resort that catered to a well-heeled clientele during the late spring and summer months. The lake was around eight kilometres in circumference and nearly 18 metres deep at the dam wall; it contained a massive volume of water. It was about 24 kilometres upstream from Johnstown.

Earth and rubble dams are normally safe provided they have been well constructed and water is never allowed to flow over the top of the wall, a requirement normally met by releasing water from the dam when the level is high by means of a spillway or an exit pipe that can be opened or closed. Somehow, because of the way this dam had evolved, South Fork did not have an efficient water-control mechanism.

The mood of the Memorial Day parade was dampened a little by the weather. Preceding days of heavy rain meant that all the rivers and creeks in the area were running full. And on the night of 30 May, the rain redoubled, with a continuous, heavy deluge developing over the upper reaches of the Little Conemaugh and across the South Fork Dam.

John Parke, the engineer employed by the Club to monitor the dam, became alarmed at the way the water level was rising. He mobilised a force of labourers to hastily dig a makeshift spillway in an attempt to let some water out. But despite their best efforts, the level continued to rise steadily.

Engineers and labourers watched, appalled, as the water swiftly rose to the top of the wall and slid over, in a smooth, fast-moving avalanche over 90 metres across. Then abruptly, at 4.07 pm on 31 May, the dam gave way. With a massive sigh, followed by a terrible roar, the lake emptied into the valley below.

A mighty wall of water swept down the Little Conemaugh, over 20 metres high in places, utterly destroying several settlements in its path. Johnstown residents became aware of a noise like continuous rolling thunder, growing louder by the minute, and were horrified by what they saw. A huge mountain of water raced towards them, roiling with houses, tree trunks, railway cars and dead livestock. It smashed into Johnstown, carrying all before it to obliterate some 1600 homes and drown 2209 people.

Despite the fact that many blamed the South Fork Fishing and Hunting Club for the disaster, no successful legal actions were ever brought against the club or any of its members.

The Dreyfus Affair

In 1894 some papers discovered by accident in a rubbish bin in Paris suggested that an unknown French army officer was spying for Germany. The subsequent investigation triggered what became one of the most sensational events in the history of France.

Alfred Dreyfus, a captain in the French army, was immediately suspected: he had access to the information in question but, more importantly, he was a Jew. There was a strong anti-Semitic undercurrent in the French army of the day, particularly at senior levels, and this counted heavily against him.

Army investigators concluded that the handwriting on the papers was similar to Dreyfus's, and he was hauled before a court martial, charged with treason. In a travesty of justice, he was denied the right to examine the evidence against him, and found guilty as charged, despite his constant protestations of innocence. In a degrading public ceremony held on 5 January 1895, he was forced to stand at attention while his epaulettes and badges of rank were torn from his uniform and his sword broken. During this ceremony he exclaimed loudly: 'You are degrading an innocent man! Long live France! Long live the army!' He was sentenced to life imprisonment and shipped off to the infamous Devils Island penal establishment off the coast of South America.

Some two years after Dreyfus's conviction, another French army officer, Lieutenant Colonel Georges Picquart, who was uneasy with the way the trial had been conducted, re-examined the evidence and concluded that in fact Dreyfus was innocent, and that another officer, Major Walsin Esterhazy, was the real spy. The army was desperate to save face, however, and Picquart's findings were totally ignored. Esterhazy was subjected to a 'show' court martial and found not guilty, despite the compelling evidence against him.

> Zola, using all his skill and eloquence, revealed the terrible injustice done to Dreyfus—the way he had been framed, the extent of the army cover-up, and the obvious guilt of Esterhazy.

A far more powerful convert to Dreyfus' cause now emerged—the famous French writer Emile Zola, who had been following the case with interest and assembling all the information he could find. Some two days after Esterhazy's not-guilty verdict, Zola burst into print in what many believe to be the greatest newspaper article ever written.

His open letter to the President of France appeared in the daily newspaper *L'Aurore* (The Dawn) on 13 January 1898 under the electrifying headline 'J'accuse!' (I Accuse!). In four thousand words, Zola, using all his skill and eloquence, revealed the terrible injustice done to Dreyfus—the way he had been framed, the extent of the army cover-up, and the obvious guilt of Esterhazy.

The article created a sensation across all of France, as well as drawing considerable outside attention because of Zola's international standing as a writer. An amazing series of events followed. The army, fearing the outcome of a retrial of Dreyfus, ordered an officer to forge additional incriminating evidence against him and attach it to his file. When later confronted with evidence of this crime, the officer concerned committed suicide. Zola was found guilty of libel and fled to England to avoid gaol. (He later returned when granted amnesty.)

In 1899 the French president officially pardoned Dreyfus, who returned to France in 1906 and was reinstated to his former military rank.

The Dreyfus affair was a sad case where entrenched interests and sectarianism were able to override a national justice system, but it was also an awesome display of the power of the press, which in this case corrected an outrageous injustice.

Portrait of Captain Alfred Dreyfus circa 1892.

A shipwreck near Tuvalu – a Pacific Island chain threatened by rising sea levels associated with global warming.

Global Warming

For over a hundred years, scientists have known that the climate of the Earth has changed many times in the past; substantial evidence points to ice ages interspersed with warmer periods over epochs extending across many thousands of years.

In Europe, for example, what is today known as the Medieval Warm Period extended from around 900 to 1350. Temperatures during this time were uncharacteristically warm across Britain and much of Eastern Europe. This was followed by the Little Ice Age, which lasted from around 1350 to 1800, a period noted for cool summers and extremely cold winters. During these four centuries, England's Thames River often froze over completely in winter, allowing markets known to the locals as the 'Frost Fairs' to be established on the ice.

These climate variations were believed to be triggered by natural causes, such as variations in the Sun's output, volcanic activity, changes in ocean currents and cyclical variations in the orbit of the Earth around the Sun. But in 1896 the Swedish scientist Svante Arrhenius raised an intriguing new possibility. He theorised that the burning of fossil fuels, particularly coal, which had been accelerating steadily since the dawn of the second Industrial Revolution in the 1850s, could eventually produce a warming of the atmosphere. The reason for this was that coal combustion produces the gas carbon dioxide, a known greenhouse gas that helps trap heat from the Sun within the Earth's atmosphere.

Arrhenius's theory was dismissed by many scientists, who argued that the effect of human activities on the atmosphere was negligible and easily outweighed by other natural processes. The concept of human influence changing the climate lay dormant for many years.

However, with improved monitoring of the atmosphere and increased cooperation between nations through the World Meteorological Organisation, scientists were able to progressively plot clearer trends in the temperature of the atmosphere, and during the 1970s and 1980s a pronounced warming trend began to emerge.

Disturbing hard evidence also accumulated, including a steady retreat of many of the world's glaciers, melting of both Arctic and Antarctic sea ice, and the increase in frequency of coral bleaching (damage to coral formations caused by an increase in the temperature of ocean waters).

However, the basic question remained—was this warming part of a natural cycle, such as was seen in the Medieval Warm Period, or was there a 'human footprint' involved? Climatologists ran repeated computer simulations, with many concluding that the temperature increases being observed could only be accounted for by a rise in concentration of greenhouse gases produced by human activity—notably carbon dioxide.

Worried governments decided to act. In 1998 the Kyoto Protocol, which required participating countries to reduce their emission of greenhouse gases below target amounts by 2012, was established. One hundred and eighty-six countries became signatories and agreed to ratify the process; the United States and Australia were notable exceptions.

Evidence of global warming continues to mount: the warmest ten years on record have all occurred since 1990; 1998 and 2005 have been rated equally as the warmest years globally in recorded history. Increases in extreme weather—another theoretical outcome of global warming—have also been observed around the world, with more frequent droughts, heat waves and severe hurricanes all being noted.

Many scientists believe that the major changes predicted by global warming are now inevitable and represent a larger threat to the future of humanity than social blights such as disease or global warfare.

A suffragette demonstration in Hyde Park, London, in 1908.

American Suffragettes in a street parade, 1917.

The Suffragettes

In 1897 Millicent Fawcett, the wife of the MP for Brighton, Henry Fawcett, began a movement called the National Union of Women's Suffrage Societies (NUWSS), dedicated to obtaining the right to vote for women in Britain.

NUWSS, a non-violent organisation, was also interested in increasing the availability of higher education for British women, but obtaining the right to vote was its main aim. The women belonging to this organisation were known as 'suffragists', from the word suffrage, literally meaning 'the right to vote'.

With NUWSS making only slow gains over the next six years, another women's group was founded in an attempt to speed up the process. This was the Women's Social and Political Union (WSPU), begun by the remarkable English women Emmeline Pankhurst and her two daughters, Christobel and Sylvia. Women in this group called themselves 'suffragettes' and, unlike their more moderate sisters in the NUWSS, were quite prepared to use violent tactics to further their cause if necessary.

Initially their efforts were peaceful, but when they felt that politicians were ignoring them, their efforts became more confrontational. They took to attending Parliament, where they heckled ministers making speeches. They held large street demonstrations involving hundreds of women, with several chaining themselves to fences to bring maximum attention their cause.

Their demonstrations became increasingly violent, with stone-throwing, physical confrontations with police, smashing of windows and, on at least one occasion, attempted arson. Much of England, and indeed Europe and America, was shocked to see otherwise respectable 'middle and upper class' women prepared to go to such lengths to further their political cause, and condemnation or approbation of their tactics resulted in a significant political divide across much of the Western world.

As the years passed, arrests and imprisonment naturally followed for the suffragettes. Many went on hunger strikes while in prison, with authorities then subjecting them to the humiliation of forced feeding, usually by means of a tube through the nostrils.

In an attempt to thwart the hunger strikes, in 1913 the British parliament passed an act called the *Prisoners, Temporary Discharge for Health Act* (known on the streets as 'The Cat and Mouse Act'). Under this law, if an individual was undertaking a hunger strike, he or she could be discharged from prison when their health deteriorated, and re-arrested at a later date when their health had improved. This saved authorities the acute embarrassment of having prisoners die in custody.

Possibly the most infamous single suffragette incident occurred in 1913, when protester Emily Davison ran out onto the racetrack during the Epsom Derby and died after being struck and trampled by a racehorse. This tragic event was captured on an early movie film and became the iconic event for the suffragette movement.

The onset of World War I in 1914 dramatically changed the situation, and the WSPU firmly endorsed the war effort, ceasing their demonstrations. With the vast bulk of young men away at the war, women earned widespread respect by taking up all the industrial work vital for the running of the country, and this added to the groundswell that demanded equal voting rights. Women over 30 were finally given the right to vote in 1918, and this was extended to the over-21 group in 1928. The efforts of Millicent Fawcett and Emmeline Pankhurst had finally been vindicated.

The Wright Brothers

Since the earliest days of history, humanity has dreamed of flying. Think of the Greek legend of Daedalus and Icarus, flying with waxen wings over the sea to escape from Crete.

Over the ensuing centuries many other imaginative and fruitless attempts were made, involving jumping off cliffs with eagles' wings attached to the body, running along flapping wooden copies of wings, or being hoisted aloft by several large kites.

Lighter-than-air flight was finally achieved in a hot-air balloon on 21 November 1783, when two French noblemen ascended 150 metres above Paris in a balloon made by the Montgolfier brothers, and flew for twenty-two minutes across the countryside.

However, what was really sought after was a heavier-than-air machine that could lift off from the ground carrying a 'pilot', be controlled in flight and land without self-destructing. The difficulties involved in producing such a device were so complex and numerous that they would not be overcome until after the dawn of the twentieth century, some 120 years after the flight of the Montgolfier balloon.

To produce such a heavier-than-air machine, an advanced understanding of aerodynamics was essential, as were considerable skills in the engineering and construction of aerodynamic surfaces. And possibly the most difficult issue was the manufacture of the power-plant that would drive the machine. By the late nineteenth century the recently invented internal combustion engine seemed to offer the most promise, but it was heavy and bulky.

These theoretical and mechanical difficulties were not solved by eminent scientists or engineers, however, but by two obscure American bicycle-shop owners, the brothers Wilbur and Orville Wright of Dayton, Ohio.

Wilbur (1867–1912) and Orville (1871–1948) Wright were the sons of Bishop Milton Wright and his wife Susan, two of a family of five living siblings. The children were strongly encouraged intellectually, having access to a large family library, and being taught the value of independent thinking.

The brothers' entrepreneurial spirit emerged early when as young men they entered into a printing business—The Wright Bros, Job Printers—after designing their own printing press. With the explosive growth of the bicycle during the late 1880s they correctly saw a new business opportunity, left the printing shop and began a new venture, the Wright Cycle Company.

Wilbur and Orville had long been interested in the possibility of powered heavier-than-air flight; when the Wright Cycle Company became financially successful, they found themselves with the time and income to begin experimentation.

They began by designing and building large unmanned gliders and from these learned how to construct control surfaces that would allow them to 'steer' the machines while flying. The extremely difficult problem of how to power their aircraft was overcome when they built their own lightweight petrol engine—it pumped out 9 kilowatts of power and weighed just over 68 kilograms—a power-to-weight ratio that made it feasible for their purpose.

They finally constructed their flying machine as what appeared to be a giant box-kite made of wood and muslin glued together and powered by two counter-rotating 'propellers' driven by their lightweight engine.

In this unlikely machine they flew into the history books on 17 December 1903 when, with Orville at the controls, it lifted off from the sands of Kitty Hawk, North Carolina, and remained aloft for about 37 metres. The ancient dream of controlled flight was finally realised with one of the most significant inventions of the human race.

The Wright brothers first flight at Kitty Hawk in 1903.

Almost immediately, scores of buildings in the central business district of San Francisco collapsed, killing numerous pedestrians and many horses on the streets below.

Massive destruction at the corner of Market and Third Street, San Francisco, 1906.

The San Francisco Earthquake

Earth's crust is composed of a jigsaw of gigantic hardened rock 'plates' that creep about over the inner core of melted rock (magma), very slowly, usually in the order of less than 25 mm a year.

Where two plates abut is known as a fault-line. This is normally an area of persistent seismic activity resulting from the friction caused by the enormous slabs of rock grinding against each other. Sometimes the movement is relatively smooth and continuous, its effects realised as frequent minor tremors causing little damage. In some regions the plates remain locked together for perhaps a hundred years or more before the strain becomes too much, and the fault lets go in a series of violent 'spasms' that can trigger major earthquakes.

Such a fault-line, the San Andreas Fault between the so-called Pacific Plate and the North American Plate, extends along the west coast of the United States, in particular across the San Francisco area. Movement across the San Andreas Fault produced one of the major earthquakes of modern history.

At around 5.13 am on 18 April 1906, several hundred kilometres of the fault-line ruptured, with the epicentre close to San Francisco itself. The resulting massive quake lasted nearly a minute, and the lateral swaying movement of the ground was so violent that pedestrians were thrown off their feet. Almost immediately, scores of buildings in the central business district of San Francisco collapsed, killing numerous pedestrians and many horses on the streets below.

Soon after the major jolts ceased, fires erupted in the debris and began to consume those buildings that remained standing. The fires were probably caused by the ignition of gas escaping from broken pipes. The water mains were also shattered, leaving firefighters severely handicapped. Desperate attempts were made to halt the spread of the flames by dynamiting buildings ahead of the blaze, but to little effect. The conflagration was so fierce that it burned out of control for another twenty-four hours, consuming whole city blocks.

There were apocalyptic scenes right across town, the city resembling a war zone with collapsed buildings, blazing ruins and people running about in screaming panic. A series of aftershocks resulted in even more buildings collapsing and spread further terror, chaos and confusion throughout the city. Additionally, huge fissures had opened up along roadways, with reports of people and animals disappearing down them at the height of the quake.

Fearing a breakdown of law and order, the authorities sent in army troops with instructions to patrol the city streets to prevent looting. The mayor, Mr E. Schmitz, issued a formal proclamation: 'The Federal Troops, the members of the Regular Police Force and all Special Police Officers have been authorised by me to KILL any and all persons found engaged in looting or in the Commission of Any Other Crime'.

Order was gradually restored by the weekend, some three days later, and it was time to count the cost. The city district had been largely flattened, as if by a giant explosion. Nearly five hundred city blocks had been levelled, about 28 000 buildings destroyed, and about a quarter of a million people had lost their homes. The death toll has never been accurately determined, but estimates in the region of two to three thousand are generally accepted.

The quake was later estimated to have reached 8.3 on the Richter scale, a rating classified as a 'great earthquake'.

People about 50 kilometres away were knocked to the ground by the shock waves from the blast, and observers further out reported hearing and feeling a series of deep concussive detonations.

A meteorite entering Earth's atmosphere at high speed.

The Tunguska Meteorite

At about 7.15 on the morning of 30 June 1908, a massive fireball was seen streaking across the blue summer sky above a remote area in central Siberia called Tunguska. Eyewitnesses, among them local settlers and reindeer herdsmen, watched as it sped towards the ground. Abruptly, before it hit, a gigantic flash lit up the sky, producing a deafening crash followed by a series of loud bangs.

People about 50 kilometres away were knocked to the ground by the shock waves from the blast, and observers further out reported hearing and feeling a series of deep concussive detonations.

The blast was picked up by seismic instruments and barographs right across western Asia and Europe, even as far away as England. While it was obvious some type of colossal explosion had taken place, it was to be many years before a satisfactory explanation of the cause emerged.

Nearly twenty years later, in 1927, the Russian geologist Leonid Kulik visited the area, hoping to verify his belief that the incident had been caused by a falling meteorite. On reaching the locality of the blast, he was astonished to find vast numbers of flattened and scorched trees pointing outward from a central zone and extending for about 50 kilometres in all directions. Closing in on the central area, he was confident he would find a large crater where the meteorite had impacted, but to his surprise found none, despite an assiduous search.

Mystified, Kulik continued his investigations for several years. In 1938 an aerial survey under his direction showed that the area of destruction was far more extensive than he had first realised. In fact over 2000 square kilometres of forest had been flattened, destroying an estimated 60 million trees. But again no crater could be located.

Other theories began to be put forward by a fascinated scientific community. Clearly there had been a phenomenal explosion across the area, with the pattern of fallen trees radiating from a central point pointing to the circular passage outwards of a massive shock wave. One feasible theory was that it must have been a fragment of a comet of considerable size, or indeed an entire small comet, that had crossed into the Earth's atmosphere. Comets are composed primarily of ice that melts after entry into the atmosphere, and this would explain why there was no crater. Opponents of this theory believed that a comet would have completely vaporised high in the atmosphere and not come close enough to the ground to create the Tunguska event.

Another theory then emerged. It was proposed that the blast had indeed been produced by a meteorite, as first thought, a meteorite composed of a conglomerate of various rocky materials and about 60 metres across. Entering the atmosphere at tremendous velocity, the 'stony' meteorite was subjected to phenomenal heat and pressure that eventually exceeded what its mixed structure could bear. This triggered an immense 'airburst explosion', estimated to have occurred at an altitude of around 6–10 kilometres above the Earth, totally destroying the meteorite. This produced the great shock-wave effect without resulting in a piece of debris large enough to blast out a surface crater. Other meteorites that are known to have generated large craters were probably not conglomerates but made of a homogeneous material such as iron, and thus able to survive intact all the way to the surface.

The Tunguska explosion is believed to have been the equivalent of a large hydrogen bomb and would certainly have demolished any city below. Scientists estimate that an event of this magnitude can be expected about once every 300 years or so.

The Sinking of the *Titanic*

The *Titanic* was, at the time of construction, the largest ocean-going vessel ever built, with an astonishing length of 270 metres and an all-up weight of nearly 47 000 tonnes. The ship had several advanced design features, including electrically powered internal waterproof doors that could be activated in the case of a hull puncture, and was powered by three massive propellers driven by reciprocating steam engines in tandem with a turbine engine—a massive powerplant for the day.

Surprisingly, the *Titanic* also contained some curious design features that would ultimately assume major significance. Firstly, the hull was of a single-layer design, whereas some of the other big ships of the era, such as the *Mauretania* and the *Lusitania*, had hulls consisting of double layers for extra strength. And strangely, the waterproof doors could not be extended as high as the deckheads—this meant that water entering faster than the pumps' capacity to remove it could fill up a waterproof compartment and then flow over the top of the electric door into the next.

The *Titanic* was to carry over 2200 people on its first voyage, but because of outdated safety regulations was only obliged to carry lifeboats for 1100 people. The possibility of the ship sinking was considered so remote that it was not awarded any serious consideration.

The luxuriously fitted out vessel, proclaimed 'unsinkable', was the jewel in the crown of the glamorous White Star Line, and the company planned a glittering social occasion for its maiden voyage from Southampton, England to New York City. The first-class passenger list consisted of a who's who of American high society, including many millionaire captains of industry together with prominent publishers, socialites and their families.

Also present was John Ismay, managing director of the White Star Line, who would accompany the captain, Edward Smith, on the bridge for part of the voyage. Ismay was anxious for publicity purposes that the *Titanic* should put up a fast time for its first transatlantic crossing, and Captain Smith was prepared for this when the ship departed on 10 April 1912. The *Titanic* entered the Atlantic the next day, and quickly increased speed to its maximum capability of 22.5 knots.

As the liner raced across the ocean, radio reports came in from other ships of icebergs along the route in unusually large numbers. The cold Labrador Current was transporting them southwards from their calving spots on the glaciers of Greenland and creating a real hazard for all shipping in the north Atlantic.

Unwilling to slow down, perhaps because of Ismay's presence on board, Captain Smith entered the ice field and maintaining high speed until, at 11.40 pm on the night of 14 April, the *Titanic* struck a large iceberg a glancing blow, ripping a large gash along the starboard side of the hull. The pumps and electric doors were immediately activated, but the pumps were unable to keep up with the inflow, and the water just overflowed from one watertight compartment to the next. The ship was doomed.

As the liner settled in the water, the passengers took to the lifeboats, unaware that there was nowhere near enough room for everyone. The ship went down at 2.20 am, with 1522 people either drowning or freezing to death in the icy waters. There were 705 survivors, rescued later in the morning from their lifeboats by the Cunard liner *Carpathia*.

The vessel proclaimed 'unsinkable', was the jewel in the crown of the White Star Line, and the company planned a glittering social occasion for its maiden voyage from Southampton, England to New York City.

The Titanic puts to sea soon after her construction was completed, and (below) slides under the waves as lifeboats struggle way from the scene.

Soldiers removing bodies from a trench at Argonne, France in 1915.

World War I Begins

During the first decade of the twentieth century many European nations were, for a variety of reasons, regarding each other with increasing mistrust. Britain, with its colonies falling into line, had forged defensive alliances with Russia and France, while Germany, Austria and Hungary formed an opposing alliance. With these complex relationships in place, it was generally hoped that the status quo could be maintained.

But the tensions were too great, and in June 1914 the dogs of war were unleashed when the heir to the Austro-Hungarian throne, Archduke Franz Ferdinand, was assassinated in Sarajevo by a member of the Serbian nationalist group known as the Black Hand.

Austria–Hungary promptly declared war on Serbia, and the alliances that had been designed to maintain peace now dragged Britain and the countries of continental Europe into the vortex. Germany invaded Belgium and France, only to become bogged down fighting the French and the British in a hideous defensive conflict—trench warfare—which resulted in hundreds of thousands of soldiers on both sides being butchered in seesawing battles that also produced dreadful tolls of wounded for gains of only a few metres of territory. Nineteenth century military thinking and tactics proved hopelessly inadequate, on both sides, in the face of the heavy artillery, machine guns and barbed wire being used on the Western Front between 1914 and 1917.

The names of the battles of this era became synonymous with human slaughter on a scale never before seen. Ypres, Verdun, the Somme, Polygon Wood, Arras and Marne reaped an increasingly grim harvest as the deadly stalemate of trench warfare continued. Frightening new weapons were tried—the aeroplane was used for the first time as an offensive weapon, and the horror of chemical warfare was introduced, with the use of gas shells that blinded and killed.

To the east, the Russians and the Germans fought other brutal battles, and British forces, including troops from Australia and New Zealand, were brought to a standstill by the Turks when the ill-fated 'forcing of the Dardanelles' was attempted.

The Allies, greatly assisted by the entry of the United States into the war, gradually obtained the upper hand and wore Germany down, but the immense losses on both sides continued to escalate. By 11 November 1918 Germany could go no further and capitulated, being forced to accept humiliating conditions of surrender. The madness was over, at least for the time being.

Sixteen million people, both soldiers and civilians, had been killed and over twenty million wounded in what was being called 'The Great War' and 'The War to End All Wars'. Europe was changed forever in a whole variety of political and social ways. In particular, a whole generation, that of the young men who had fought and died, or survived with debilitating injuries, had become highly cynical about life, religion and unquestioning patriotism.

The cynicism and unease is powerfully revealed in some of the literature that emerged from the war. Erich Maria Remarque's classic *All Quiet on the Western Front*, the story of a German infantryman, is strongly anti-war in sentiment. On the British side, the haunting poetry of Wilfred Owen, a British officer killed just before Armistice Day, achieved widespread renown.

THE NEW YORK HERALD.

PART II.　　　NEW YORK, SATURDAY, MAY 8, 1915.—TWENTY-TWO PAGES.—BY THE NEW YORK HERALD COMPANY.　　****　　PRICE THREE CENTS.

THE LUSITANIA IS SUNK;
1,000 PROBABLY ARE LOST

LAST PICTURE OF THE LUSITANIA TAKEN AS SHE LEFT NEW YORK HARBOR.

CAPTAIN WILLIAM T. TURNER, OF THE LUSITANIA

ALFRED G. VANDERBILT

ELBERT HUBBARD

CHARLES FROHMAN

JUSTUS MILES FORMAN

CHARLES KLEIN

GERMANS TORPEDO THE GIANT STEAMSHIP AND SHE FOUNDERS EIGHT MILES FROM IRISH COAST

Ten Boats Are Lowered and Officers Work Heroically, but Inrush of Water Through Great Holes in Vessel's Bottom Sends Her Down, Bow First, in Twenty Minutes.

TWO FEARFUL MISSILES TEAR THROUGH SIDE NEAR BOW AND AT THE ENGINE ROOM

Great Ship Is Nearing St. George's Channel as the Unseen Enemy Launches Torpedoes That Bend Her Hull.

[Special Cable to the Herald.]

Herald Bureau, No. 130 Fleet Street, London, Saturday.

The steamship Lusitania, of the Cunard line, one of the largest and finest vessels in the world, was nearing the entrance to St. George's Channel, between the Irish and English coasts, yesterday afternoon with 1,254 passengers from New York and a crew of 816, when an unseen German submarine discharged two torpedoes which struck her and sent her to the bottom in twenty minutes.

One of the chief officers of the Lusitania, F. V. Jones, has informed the Admiralty that he believes between 500 and 600 persons, including passengers and crew, have been saved. More conservative estimates by survivors place the loss at a thousand.

The great steamship when the torpedoes found their target trembled a moment under the shock. Her engines stopped and the seas poured in through the tremendous rent in her hull.

As the Lusitania listed far over, and as her wireless apparatus sent frantic appeals for aid, the crew manned the lifeboats and ten, already prepared and in readiness for instant use, were lowered, all filled with passengers.

The tug Storm Cock reached Queenstown early this morning with about one hundred and fifty survivors, principally passengers, among whom were many women, several of the crew and one steward. Describing the experience of the Lusitania, the steward said:—

The passengers were at lunch when a submarine came up and fired two torpedoes, which struck the Lusitania on the starboard side, one forward and the other in the engine room. They caused terrific explosions.

"Captain Turner immediately ordered the boats out. The ship began to list badly immediately.

TEN BOATS PUT INTO WATER.

"Ten boats were put into the water, and between 400 and 500 passengers were saved. Our boat approached the land with three other boats and we were picked up just after four o'clock by the Storm Cock.

"I fear that few of the officers were saved. They acted bravely.

"There was only fifteen minutes from the time the ship was struck until she foundered, going down bow foremost. It was a dreadful sight."

Two other steamships with survivors are approaching Queenstown.

The greatest interest concerning the action to be taken by the United States government was felt in official circles here last night. There seems to be little doubt that the lives of many Americans

George A. Kessler One of Those Saved, Cable Message to Cunard Office Says

At ten minutes after eleven o'clock last night officers of the Cunard line in this city announced that cable messages were being received from London and Liverpool giving names and addresses of the survivors. The work of obtaining the names is very tedious; it was announced, and great pains are being taken to see that they are correct.

The first message received was from Liverpool and was as follows:—

"GENERAL LASSETTER'S WIFE AND SON ARE SAFE."

The next message read:—

"MRS. J. T. SMITH, OF BRACEVILLE, OHIO, AND MR. GEORGE A. KESSLER, OF NEW YORK CITY, BOTH ARE SAFE."

Just before the Cunard offices closed for the night a cable message announced:—

"MISS IRENE PAYNTER IS SAVED."

No mention was made of Charles E. Paynter, of Liverpool, father of Miss Paynter.

The Lassetters referred to in the first message are evidently Mrs. H. B. Lassetter and F. Lassetter, both of which names appear on the Lusitania's passenger list.

The General Lassetter referred to is probably Colonel Harry Beauchamp Lassetter, who was made a Commander of the Bath in 1902. He is a son of F. Lassetter, of Sydney, Australia. He was married in 1891 to Miss Elizabeth Antill and has one son, who is evidently the F. Lassetter of the passenger list. Colonel Lassetter has a record for distinguished service in Australia, Egypt and South Africa. His wife and son, it is said, had been with friends in Los Angeles, Cal.

Mr. Kessler is an importer of champagnes and is well known in New York, London and Paris.

citizens have been sacrificed in this latest assault of the German under sea raiders on British commerce.

Late despatches to the Admiralty last night stated that the survivors are being landed and that the wounded are being sent to the naval and military hospitals. The only persons identified as saved are General Lassiger and son (first cabin) and Mrs. Bretherton (second cabin). The Cunard line made their names public this morning.

There is no doubt here to-night that many of the passengers and crew were wounded by the explosion of the torpedos. The vessel was sunk early in the afternoon in a great sea, and the water, while chilly,

was not cold enough to cause suffering by exposure. As the despatches from Queenstown specifically mention the wounded, it is inferred that their wounds were inflicted by the explosion of the torpedos.

No word is obtainable concerning the fate of the prominent persons who left New York on board the Lusitania. These included Mr. Alfred G. Vanderbilt, Mr. Charles Frohman, Mr. Justus Miles Forman, Mr. Charles Klein, Mr. and Mrs. Elbert Hubbard and Mr. Julian de Ayala, Cuban Consul General at Liverpool.

The Lusitania was due to arrive at Liverpool last evening. She was near the entrance to St. George's

RESCUE VESSELS SPEED TO THE SCENE TO PICK UP SURVIVORS; ONLY 500 ARE ACCOUNTED FOR

Wireless Call for Help Is Caught by Many Passing Craft and Land Stations, but Naval Observer Ashore Sees Ship Disappear Before Aid Can Reach Her.

TUG ARRIVES AT QUEENSTOWN WITH 150 SURVIVORS FOUND IN BOATS

Numerous Distinguished Passengers Aboard, but No List of Saved Can Be Obtained—Rescued Are Hurried to Hospitals and Many Are Reported Dead from Injuries.

1,000 LIVES LOST, LAST ESTIMATE.

London, Saturday, 4:54 A. M.

A DUBLIN despatch to the Exchange Telegraph Company says the latest reports indicate a loss of life on the Lusitania of about one thousand.

Channel, leading to the Irish Sea, in which German submarines have been reported recently, and was proceeding to her destination when the submarine crept upon her, and, according to the officers of the Cunard line, without warning fired the torpedo at her hull.

From the fact that latest advices say the giantess of the seas sank within twenty minutes or twenty-one minutes some idea can be gained of the size of the great holes opened in her hull.

The Titanic, of the White Star line, remained afloat two hours after the hull had been pierced by an iceberg, and as the Lusitania went to the bottom so quickly it is believed her hull was damaged much more extensively than was that of the Titanic.

Not a word has come from Ireland concerning the submarine that wrought the awful havoc. Apparently the death dealing craft concealed herself beneath the surface of the water and escaped unseen.

WIRELESS CATCHES APPEAL FOR HELP.

The first information that the Lusitania had been torpedoed came from the wireless station at Old Head, Kinsale, on the Irish coast. The marine observer there had seen the steamship stop and list badly. The wireless operator then picked up this message from the Lusitania:—

"Send help quickly. Am listing badly."

Half a dozen vessels were hurried out from Kinsale to where the Lusitania was lying helpless. She was then eight miles south by west from Kinsale. The first message was received about twelve minutes after two o'clock. All reports agree that the Lusitania suddenly plunged to the bottom at thirty-three minutes after two o'clock. Therefore she was afloat only twenty or twenty-one minutes after she had been torpedoed. In that brief time the lifeboats on board had to be launched, and, it is reported from Kinsale, that they were put into the sea crowded with passengers.

So brief was the period given to the 2,070 persons on board to

New York Herald headlines announce the sinking of the Lusitania, *May 1915.*

Torpedoing of the
Lusitania

The *Lusitania* was a luxury ocean liner used on the lucrative transatlantic run between England and America during the early years of the twentieth century. With a magnificently appointed interior and superbly serviced by a dedicated crew, the liner was a great favourite with passengers, and along with its elegant sister ship, the *Mauretania*, carried the flag of the mighty Cunard Line with great distinction.

The *Lusitania* was fast, and also highly manoeuvrable for such a big ship, and first broke the transatlantic record—winning the much sought-after Blue Riband—in October 1907, with an average speed just a tick under 24 knots.

When World War I erupted across Europe some seven years later, there were many in America who wanted to directly assist England—and many who opposed the idea. The United States decided on a course of neutrality, but watched the developments in Europe with growing concern.

One of the German command's first ploys against Britain was to attempt a blockade by sea, with the intent of cutting off much-needed supplies of food and war ordnance. One of the most potent weapons in the sea war was the German submarine—or U-Boat—that began wreaking havoc on Atlantic shipping during 1915. The transatlantic run became increasingly dangerous. Ships' captains were advised to proceed at full throttle and to perform numerous random zigzags en route to prevent being lined up by a marauding U-Boat.

On 1 May 1915, the *Lusitania* departed New York for Liverpool in England, carrying nearly 2000 passengers, including 159 Americans. Travelling at full speed for the next six days, the liner arrived off the Irish coast on the early afternoon of 7 May, but was forced to slow down because of thick fog in the area. This enabled the lurking German submarine U-20 to take aim and fire a torpedo which streaked into the starboard side of the *Lusitania*, triggering a massive explosion followed

soon after by an even more massive blast.

The *Lusitania* went down in a little over fifteen minutes, with around 1200 people, including 128 Americans, dying in the attack. The world was shocked at the scale of the tragedy, as well as by the concept of a ship of war attacking an unarmed passenger vessel. The United States, in particular, was outraged, and the event immediately soured relations with Germany. The US government stated that the attack on the *Lusitania* 'was contrary to international law and the conventions of all civilized nations'.

Great controversy erupted about the second explosion. The U-Boat's commander, Captain Walter Schweiger, was adamant that he had fired only one torpedo and that the other blast must have come from within the liner itself, perhaps from the ignition of coal dust around the steam engines. The German government went further, claiming that the *Lusitania* had been illegally carrying a secret cargo of munitions to assist the British war effort, and was therefore a legitimate military target.

Although a military victory for Germany, the attack was a diplomatic and public relations disaster of colossal proportions, with the British portraying the German military as inhuman monsters, and public opinion in America turning distinctly anti-German.

More significantly, it probably played a major role in the decision of the United States to enter the war in 1917, with the defeat of Germany then virtually guaranteed.

The Battle of Jutland

In 1916 the capital ship of any naval fleet was the battleship—a steel leviathan encased in armourplate and carrying as much firepower as possible, frequently eight 305 millimetre guns and capable of a top speed in excess of 20 knots.

The strength of a navy was measured by how many of these monsters a country had in its fleet. A great battleship-building race began during the early 1900s, mainly involving Britain and Germany. Germany's Kaiser Wilhelm and Admiral von Tirpitz beefed up the strength of the German navy through the establishment of an energetic ship-building program.

The British constructed what became the yardstick for all future battleships of the era— *HMS Dreadnought*, launched in 1906. This vessel was a technological breakthrough, powered by steam turbine engines instead of the older and slower triple-expansion powerplants, and carrying as many big guns as physically possible. 'Dreadnought' became the generic name for all similar battleships—others were known as 'pre-dreadnoughts'.

Both Britain and Germany had several 'dreadnoughts' in their fleets at the start of World War I, and both sides anticipated that a great and decisive naval battle would be fought with these massive warships.

It appeared that the time had arrived on 31 May 1916, when the German Navy laid a trap for British Vice-Admiral Beatty's battlecruiser squadron by luring it into the range of their main force—the High Seas Fleet. Their intentions were known to the British, however, for they had cracked the German naval code. As British Vice-Admiral Beatty appeared to flee with his force, he was in fact dragging the pursuing Germans into the range of the awaiting Royal Navy's Grand Fleet, commanded by Admiral Sir John Jellicoe.

> As British Vice-Admiral Beatty appeared to flee with his force, he was in fact dragging the pursuing Germans into the range of the awaiting Royal Navy's Grand Fleet.

The British had assembled a force consisting of twenty-eight dreadnoughts and nine battlecruisers, while the Germans, somewhat outgunned, had sixteen dreadnoughts, five battlecruisers and six pre-dreadnought vessels.

The two fleets clashed off the coast of Denmark, near Jutland, at about 6.30 pm on 31 May, with a murderous running battle ensuing for the next two hours.

The Germans were caught by surprise when the British heavy guns opened fire, and attempted to retreat. Jellicoe cut off this manoeuvre and fired furious broadsides at the German fleet for a 10-minute period, inflicting heavy damage. The Germans replied with an accurate bombardment, scoring their own series of telling hits.

Finally managing to disengage from the battle, the German fleet retreated under cover of nightfall, but with intense gunfire continuing in the darkness. At daylight, with the battle over, it was time to count the cost.

Despite his larger fleet, Jellicoe had in fact suffered heavier losses, losing three battlecruisers and thirteen smaller vessels. The Germans had lost one battlecruiser, one pre-dreadnought and nine smaller warships. The British didn't realise at the time that several of the German dreadnoughts had been severely damaged, and the High Seas Fleet was laid up in port for much of the remainder of the war.

Jutland was the greatest naval battle of World War I. It was also the last 'pure' battleship clash—in which no aircraft or submarines were involved—in history.

Commander of the Royal Navy's Grand Fleet, Admiral Sir John Jellicoe.

A British tank near the front line in France circa 1917.

A British Mark IV tank acting as a transport vehicle, circa 1917.

The Battle of Cambrai

During 1915 and 1916, the stalemate on the Western Front continued, with hundreds of thousands of young men being regularly slaughtered to gain just a few yards of territory. The terrifying new weapons of the machine gun and high explosive shell had forced the men of the battlefield to 'go underground', living in abysmal conditions in trenches dug across hundreds of kilometres of France and Belgium.

Sometime during this period, a group of innovative Englishmen set about finding a solution to the terrible deadlock. The concept of a 'land battleship' was born—an armoured machine, carrying as much firepower as possible, that could traverse the battlefield, cross trenches and break the enemy lines.

Working in top secret, the first 'tanks', so named to conceal their purpose from any German spies, were produced. These primitive armoured vehicles each carried several machine guns and were powered by a 105 hp Daimler engine driving two massive 'caterpillar tracks'. The tracks enabled the machine to travel across far rougher country than any traditional wheeled vehicle could attempt.

The tanks were tried in combat for the first time in 1916, as part of the Battle of the Somme. Only a small force was deployed, with disappointing results, but the British did not lose faith in their invention. It was eventually decided to attempt a mass attack at another point, spearheaded by a much larger number of tanks.

In the darkness just before dawn on 20 November 1917, 476 British tanks, together with a large force of infantry, gathered along a 10-kilometre front facing the German trenches near the northern French township of Cambrai to launch the first massed tank assault in history.

The Germans awoke to the rising growl of engines, and peering out into the gloom of first light were astonished to see a mass of monster machines rolling towards them across no-man's-land, with machine-gun fire crackling from their sides. To their horror, the Germans discovered that their own small-arms fire had absolutely no effect on the armour-plated leviathans, which continued their advance virtually unimpeded over broken ground and through barbed wire entanglements.

Many German troops deserted their trenches and retreated in panic towards the reserve lines, only to be overrun there as the tanks continued their remorseless advance. Combined with the large infantry force, the tanks effected a major breakthrough of the German lines, punching a breach some 5.6 kilometres deep into enemy territory. In an era where an advance of 90 metres was big news, this was truly a sensational event.

There was a problem, however. The British commanders, entirely unused to the concept of a quick advance, had not planned for fuel resupply, nor for the provision of spare parts, and the attack lost vital momentum. Subsequently the Germans were able to recapture much of the lost territory.

Despite the inconclusive outcome, the dramatic debut of the massed tank attack made a deep impression on military thinkers on both sides. Over the next twenty years, a great deal of development went into this type of vehicle. By the outbreak of World War II in 1939 the tank had evolved into a highly effective, marauding fighting machine, which would have a great impact on all future land battles.

> Many German troops deserted their trenches and retreated in panic towards the reserve lines, only to be overrun there as the tanks continued their remorseless advance.

An outdoor hospital for influenza victims, Lawrence, Massachusetts, 1918.

Two men wearing 'flu masks' in Paris, March 1919.

Spanish Influenza

As a large part of the world's population emerged from the horrors of World War I, many thought that the worst was over; that nothing could remotely approach the terrible ordeal they had just been through. But they were wrong.

Early in 1918 a highly infectious and virulent form of influenza suddenly arrived on the world stage. Appearing to erupt in Europe, its spread was assisted by the movements of troops returning home from the war. It moved with great speed, reaching every continent and producing a death toll far exceeding the devastating figures of World War I.

The influenza became known as the 'Spanish flu' because it was believed at the time that the disease had started in Spain. Modern research does not support this theory. It is more probable that its early reporting in Spain was due to the fact that Spanish newspapers were not heavily censored in what they could report at a time when most other European newspapers were.

There was no effective treatment. Doctors the world over watched helplessly as victims swiftly declined, sometimes racing from a state of 'no symptoms' to death in only a few hours. The appalling way in which they died was no less frightening than the global march of the disease itself. Victims rapidly developed acute pneumonia as their lungs filled with a viscous, bloody froth that sometimes gushed from their mouth and nose. Increasingly they had to gasp for breath until the stage was reached where they literally drowned in their own bodily fluids.

The pattern of infection was unlike anything experienced previously. Normally, influenza targets the more vulnerable members of the population—the very young and the very old, and those with existing diseases. But in this case the main victims—the 20- to 40-year age group—seemed to be in robust health and in the prime of life.

The high fatality rate, or morbidity, of the disease was particularly alarming. Previous epidemics produced death rates of around one person for every 1000 infections; Spanish flu generated the frightening figure of around 25 deaths per 1000 infections—that is, about 25 times more potent. Death rates reported across India were even worse—up to 40 fatalities for every 1000 infections.

The flu's effects were felt right around the globe, with authorities actively discouraging public gatherings in a desperate attempt to halt the progress of the disease. People were obliged to wear gauze masks when out and about in the streets, theatres were closed, store sales were banned, and hospitals overwhelmed. Undertakers were unable to keep up with the demand for their services, and there was a shortage of coffins as the death rate rose across several continents. It was said the situation was not unlike that in medieval Europe at the height of the Black Plague.

By the time the worst of the pandemic was over, late in 1919, it was estimated that around 20 to 40 million people had died, making it just as bad, if not worse, than the Plague, when an estimated 25 million had lost their lives.

Even in modern times the threat posed by the outbreak of a similar infectious disease cannot be ignored, and world health authorities closely monitor any suspected outbreak of influenza-type diseases.

> Doctors the world over watched helplessly as victims swiftly declined, sometimes racing from a state of 'no symptoms' to death in only a few hours.

American Prohibition

The temperance movement began to gather momentum across America early in the twentieth century, with the sale of alcohol prohibited in several states. The United States was emerging from the frontier era, but heavy drinking remained part of the culture in many areas. Over-consumption of alcohol was perceived by many to be the root cause of numerous financial and social ills of the times.

By 1905, three American states had already outlawed alcohol, and by 1916 Prohibition was in force across 26 of the 48 states. Following the passing of the Volstead Act, Prohibition was proclaimed right across the country on 16 January 1920. The stage was set for one of the most infamous decades in America's history—the Roaring Twenties.

Far from solving many of society's problems, Prohibition seemed to create many more. The demand for social alcohol remained strong, and its manufacture, marketing and distribution were taken over by a diverse band of criminals known as 'bootleggers', accompanied by the sinister emergence of organised crime networks.

Major cities became battlegrounds as various bootlegger gangs fought each other and the law for their share of the lucrative profits from the illegal alcohol market. Criminals murdered each other, as well as innocent citizens, with knives, pistols, tommy-guns and bombs, as corruption, extortion and bribery flourished across the nation. Sleazy 'speakeasies'—illegal clubs in which patrons could buy alcohol—were often supplied by a particular gang who would also demand 'protection money' from the owners. Rival gangs would often try and take these distribution points over, leading to murderous retributions.

One of the main weapons enthusiastically adopted by the various city mobs was the so-called tommy-gun, more properly the Thompson submachine gun. This was the brainchild of an American army general,

J.T. Thompson, who, as a result of viewing the trench conflicts of World War I, had invented a light, hand-held machine gun that produced devastating firepower and could be operated by one man in a very enclosed space. It was embraced with delight by the bootleggers, who found it ideal for shooting up restaurants, warehouses, rival mobsters and, on occasion, even pursuing police forces.

Chicago in particular developed a lawless reputation, chiefly because of the activities of the notorious mobster Al 'Scarface' Capone, who maintained order in his empire through a reign of terror, beatings and murder. In 1929 Capone was at war with rival mobster George 'Bugs' Moran, an enmity which culminated in the infamous St Valentine's Day massacre of 14 February 1929. Disguised as police, Capone's men raided a warehouse owned by Moran and cold-bloodedly executed seven of his men, creating a wave of revulsion that ultimately caused a backlash against Capone specifically, but also against Prohibition in general.

Public agitation against Prohibition gradually mounted as it became apparent that the depths of corruption and violence triggered by the Volstead Act were far more damaging to American society than the evils of 'Demon Drink' itself.

With the enthusiastic support of much of the population, the Volstead Act was finally repealed on 7 April 1933. A unique attempt by society to 'make man moral by law' had spectacularly failed.

Criminals murdered each other, as well as innocent citizens, with knives, pistols, tommy-guns and bombs, as corruption, extortion and bribery flourished across the nation.

Federal agents destroying barrels of illegal liquor, San Francisco, 1927.

The cover of an official Ku Klux Klan brochure, Atlanta, 1916.

The Rise of the Ku Klux Klan

The brotherhood of the Ku Klux Klan had its roots in the defeat of the Confederacy at the end of the American Civil War, and originally consisted of Southern veterans trying to maintain their previous way of life. The name was derived from the Greek kuklos, 'circle', combined with the English word 'clan'. Founded in 1865–66, the Klan vigorously advocated white supremacy, and was strongly anti-Republican, anti-North, anti-Semitic and anti-Catholic.

The Klansmen resorted to violence to back up their beliefs, and were responsible for thousands of beatings and lynchings during 1867 and 1868, mainly directed against blacks and white Republican voters, who were despised as black sympathisers. There was considerable public backlash against this barbarism, and President Ulysses S. Grant successfully outlawed the organisation with the passage of the Civil Rights Act of 1871.

The Ku Klux Klan remained dormant until 1915, when the 'second Klan' was born, this time attaining a certain amount of 'respectability' in large areas of the South. Its general principles were still the same, with a strong promotion of white fundamentalist Protestantism, and a vitriolic hatred of black Americans who sought equal rights. Rallies were held beneath burning crosses, attended by members wearing white hoods and robes to disguise their identities, particularly important for those who were involved in the beatings and lynchings of the people they despised.

Despite its illegal activities, the Klan attracted considerable popular support during the 1920s, with many prominent citizens, including politicians and lawmakers, becoming paid-up members. The power of the Klan probably reached its zenith during this time, spreading terror and confusion across large parts of the South, and generating a high degree of racial tension that would last for decades to come.

This community support waned considerably during World War II, when the Klan's support for the German Nazis, with their common belief in Aryan (white) supremacy, was patently at odds with the national war effort, which ironically was being assisted greatly by black American soldiers.

In more modern times the Klan became increasingly isolated, but still managed to maintain a presence in the South. There was a resurgence of activity during the Civil Rights campaigns of the 1960s, culminating in the infamous murders of three civil rights workers in 1964, allegedly by members of the Klan.

Michael Schwerner, Andy Goodman and James Chaney were campaigning for the registration of black voters in Mississippi, during the so-called 'Freedom Summer', when they were abducted at gunpoint, shot, and buried near a dam, where their bodies were later found. The murders outraged much of America, but instead of terrorising the vote registration workers as was intended, they ended up adding considerable momentum to the civil rights movement.

From the outset, Klan members were the prime suspects, in particular a local Baptist preacher and high-ranking Klansman, Edgar Ray Killen, but no proof was available at the time and no charges were laid. The incident eventually formed the basis for the 1988 movie, *Mississippi Burning*. In 2005—some 41 years after the event—Killen, at 80 years of age, was eventually arrested for manslaughter in connection with the case. He was found guilty and imprisoned in what was seen as a long-awaited victory for civil rights in the South.

During the 1930s Stalin conducted extensive purges of his political enemies, and indeed of anyone he perceived as a future threat, ordering mass arrests, executions and deportation to labour camps in Siberia.

An official portrait of Joseph Stalin, leader of the USSR, circa 1945.

The Stalinist Era

Joseph Stalin (1878–1953) was, without doubt, one of the most influential—and unpleasant—men of the twentieth century. Born Josef Vissarionovich Dzhugashvili into humble origins in the strictly controlled Russia of the tsars, he was the victim of frequent beatings by a violent and drunken father, a background said by some to account for his brutal and merciless conduct later in life.

As a schoolboy he won a scholarship to a religious seminary, where he showed a strong interest in Marxism during his secondary school years, a dangerous interest in tsarist Russia. In 1902, as a consequence of his underground activities on behalf of downtrodden workers, the budding revolutionary was arrested for distributing Marxist literature and the next year sent to Siberia in exile.

Around 1910 he changed his name to Stalin, meaning 'man of steel'. He joined the Bolsheviks in 1912, and became a permanent member of the all-powerful Politburo in 1917. Soon after the October Revolution, in 1922, he became general secretary of the Communist Party. His rise to absolute power was rapid after that, and after winning a successful power struggle against Trotsky, Stalin became the undisputed leader of the USSR in 1929.

With now untrammelled power, he began implementing his version of Marxist–Leninist philosophy, which he further developed into a political and economic system later called Stalinism. One of his strong beliefs was the value of collective farming. This much-hated policy was brutally implemented, with millions of peasant farmers displaced and hundreds of thousands dying in violent repressions of any who resisted collectivisation.

During the 1930s Stalin conducted extensive purges of his political enemies, and indeed of anyone he perceived as a future threat, ordering mass arrests, executions and deportation to labour camps in Siberia. Such ruthlessness to further consolidate his power created increasing unease in the West.

In 1938, just before the beginning of World War II, Stalin signed a non-aggression pact with Hitler, designed to keep the USSR out of the upcoming conflict. The two leaders soon fell out, however, and Germany began an invasion of the USSR in June of 1941 with the launch of Operation Barbarossa.

The German advance was rapid until the epic battle of Stalingrad, in which the Red Army crushed the German forces and turned the tide of the war. (Stalin, as head of the USSR and war leader, had ordered that no women or children were allowed to be evacuated from the city, cynically reasoning that this would make his soldiers fight harder.)

By the end of the war, the influence of the Soviet Union had greatly increased, with the Communists now dominating much of central and eastern Europe, including East Germany. This situation greatly disturbed the West, particularly the USA, and sowed the seeds of the long running 'Cold War' of later years. The USA and the USSR were now the two major world powers, the latter's rise to this status the result of Stalin's policies of industrialisation and modernisation of Russia's feudal peasant farming economy.

Despite his outwards appearance as genial and avuncular, Stalin was a brutal dictator, utterly ruthless in his determination to hold onto power at all costs. Later analyses revealed that he was responsible for the death or imprisonment of probably millions of Soviet citizens. The Stalinist era finally ended with his death in 1953.

The Tri-State Tornado

Tornados, or 'twisters', are violently rotating funnels of air spawned by severe thunderstorm activity, and are capable of producing extreme winds in excess of 485 kilometres an hour. This level of severity can result in catastrophic damage to even the strongest buildings, and is capable of flinging houses off their foundations, and hurling automobiles, people, animals and trees through the air for considerable distances.

The flying debris produced by tornados is frequently lethal to anyone caught in the open. Many people have also been killed by structural collapse when seeking shelter inside a building or mobile home unable to withstand the tornado's force.

'Tornado Alley' in the United States is the world's twister hotspot; it covers parts of Texas, Oklahoma, Kansas, Nebraska, Illinois, Missouri and Indiana. This is the rolling open country of the Great Plains, where cold air streaming south from Canada can collide with warm, humid air moving up from the Gulf of Mexico to generate lines of massive, severe thunderstorms, together with their violent tornadic offspring. This set of circumstances can occur almost any time, but is most common during the months of spring and summer.

Perhaps the most infamous and extreme event of this type ever recorded occurred on 18 March 1925, when a severe thunderstorm developed across south-east Missouri and generated a particularly violent twister. This turned out to be unlike any other tornado encountered before or since. It cut an unparalleled swathe of death and destruction across three states before finally dissipating over 350 kilometres from its place of origin. This was the deadly Tri-State Tornado, the TST.

A 'normal' twister lasts only a fairly short time, typically around half an hour or so. But TST was different—it lasted about three and half hours, producing an extended period of almost continuous destruction as it ripped its way across the countryside, travelling at speeds of up to 100 kilometres an hour. The wind speed inside the funnel itself was estimated to have been toward the top end of the tornado scale, with later analysis of the damage trail indicating possible winds around 485 kilometres an hour.

TST ripped through some twenty sizeable townships, including Gorham, Murphysboro, DeSoto, West Frankfort and Parrish, all in southern Illinois, killing a total of 488 people, and causing utter destruction right across the area. Parrish was so completely devastated that it was never rebuilt, while contemporary photographs taken in some of the other areas show settlements that closely resemble some of the French and Belgian villages destroyed by shellfire in World War I.

Eventually the tornado crossed the border into Indiana, where it inflicted massive damage to the townships of Griffin and Princeton, before finally abating after the longest continuous rampage of any known twister.

Perhaps most tragically, because it was a Wednesday, school was in and several schoolhouses were directly hit, with seventeen students dying in Murphysboro and another 33 at DeSoto. In all, 695 people died—still the record by far for an American tornado—over 2000 were injured and some 15 000 homes were demolished.

Subsequent investigation of the twister's path revealed a monstrous gouge of destruction across the countryside, some 350 kilometres long and about 1.2 kilometres wide.

The Tri-State Tornado remains the benchmark of severity against which all US tornadoes are measured. It is a perpetual reminder of how deadly a twister can become under the right conditions.

Two children sit amid the ruins of their former home.

The tornado produced scenes similar to a war zone across many areas.

The wreckage of the north wing of Bath school.

The Bath School Massacre

Andrew Kehoe was known by his neighbours to be a little eccentric, but apart from that, he and his wife seemed to be good citizens who quietly worked their small farm outside the sleepy rural township of Bath in Michigan during the first half of the 1920s. He had some odd habits, such as a desire for excessive cleanliness, and a predilection bordering on obsessiveness for tinkering with machinery; more darkly, he had a reputation for cruelty to his farm animals.

Kehoe was not a very efficient farmer. He struggled to put food on the table and keep up with the farm mortgage payments that were a constant source of worry and irritation. His financial situation worsened when extra taxes were levied to pay for the maintenance and support of the local school. As he fell further behind in his mortgage payments, he received notice that the bank was about to foreclose on his loan, increasing his smouldering resentment of the school that he believed to be the root cause of his financial problems.

Over an extended period he began amassing a stockpile of explosives, purchasing only small quantities at a time to avoid suspicion, and telling the vendors that he was using them to blow up tree stumps around his property. And indeed this was a common rural practice of the time, employing either dynamite or a substance called pyrotol that had been used during World War I. Kehoe gradually amassed large quantities of both. During the spring of 1927, he secretly stored them beneath the floor of the school building, using his position as part-time odd jobs and maintenance man as a cover for his activities.

On the morning of 18 May 1927, Kehoe, by now completely demented, put his dastardly plan into action. He first killed his wife by beating her over the head with a heavy blunt object. Then, to act as a diversion, he set fire to his farmhouse, the rising smoke soon attracting the attention of the local fire brigade that rushed to the farm.

Kehoe then set off a timed detonator attached to the explosives under the school, and took off in his car, which he had also packed with explosives and metal objects to act as shrapnel. A thunderous blast totally destroyed one of the two wings of the school, killing many children inside immediately. Several bodies were blown entirely out of the building through the roof.

A little later, as shocked rescuers gathered around the rubble of the north wing and began looking for survivors, Kehoe returned and detonated the explosives inside his car, killing himself immediately, along with several people nearby, who were shredded with shrapnel from the massive blast.

The township reeled from the terrible toll. The two blasts had killed forty-five people and injured a further fifty-eight, many seriously. Most of the victims of the first bomb were school pupils, youngsters between seven and twelve years of age, but two teachers were also killed; another five adults, including Kehoe himself, perished as a result of the car bomb.

Subsequent investigations revealed another huge cache of explosives stashed under the south wing of the school and also rigged for detonation, which had thankfully failed to explode.

The tragedy at Bath remains the deadliest school mass murder in US history, even eclipsing the terrible events at Columbine, some seventy-two years later in 1999.

Anxious crowds gather outside the New York Stock Exchange on 31 October 1929.

Panicky investors flood the streets of New York as news of the crash spreads.

Mounted body of a thylacine at the Australian Museum in Sydney.

Another view of the body of a thylacine showing the tiger-like stripes covering the hindquarters.

The ruins of Nanking railway station after a Japanese bombing raid.

Japan Invades China

In 1937 China had the world's biggest population but lacked a sense of national unity. Continuing conflict between the official Nationalist government, headed by Chiang Kai-shek, and the Communist forces led by the charismatic Mao Zedong, combined with extended periods of foreign intervention in the decades before, had weakened the nation.

This fact had not been overlooked by Japan—a country that had been adopting an increasingly imperialistic and expansionist policy, particularly under War Minister Hideki Tojo in the late 1930s, with the tacit blessing of the Emperor Hirohito.

In 1931, Japanese secret agents had staged a bomb blast on an express train in Manchuria as a pretext for invading and then occupying the region. The situation simmered for another six years until the 'Marco Polo incident' of July 1937, when Japanese and Chinese troops clashed at the Marco Polo Bridge near Peking.

This clash created the excuse Japan had been looking for, and a full-scale invasion of China was launched soon afterwards, with Japanese troops crossing into the northern areas of China from Manchuria. Massive aerial bombing raids were launched against Shanghai and Nanking, both densely populated cities, with resulting immense loss of life. At that time Nanking was the capital of China, and as such became the main object of attack by the invading Japanese army. The Nationalist forces of Chiang Kai-shek, assisted by Mao's Communists, fought back bravely, causing unexpectedly high casualties among the Japanese forces and considerably delaying their progress.

Nonetheless the inevitable occurred, and the Imperial Japanese Army finally crashed through and captured Nanking in December of 1937, little more than five months after the invasion had begun. What followed became known as the Rape of Nanking, one of history's most shocking incidents. An estimated 350 000 Chinese, both civilians and soldiers, were slaughtered following the surrender of the city, and many thousands of women and girls brutally raped.

The terrible death toll involved mass beheadings, disembowelments, bayonetings and mutilations on an unimaginable scale. To complete the degradation of the ancient and beautiful city, it was savagely bombed, burned and looted, producing damage that would take many years to overcome.

The brutal way in which Japan treated the residents of Nanking would be repeated in various degrees across much of Asia over the next eight years as the Imperial Japanese Army pushed southwards through the Philippines, Thailand and Malaya, to be stopped only in New Guinea, on the doorstep of Australia.

The period of Japanese occupation of China, from 1937 to the end of World War II in 1945, resulted in a dreadful death toll, estimated by some historians to be around 10 million people. This figure includes not only the victims of aerial bombing and ground attacks, but also the victims of starvation and disease following the occupation.

The scale of the disaster was not well reported at the time, at least in comparison with the European situation, partly because of the lack of communication between China and the West following the rise to power of Mao Zedong after the end of World War II.

> Massive aerial bombing raids were launched against Shanghai and Nanking, both densely populated cities, with resulting immense loss of life.

The Hindenburg *flying over New York just before its disastrous attempt to dock at nearby Lakehurst Field.*

The Crash of the *Hindenburg*

'Dirigible' is the engineering term used to describe a lighter-than-air balloon (airship) that carries engines to allow steering and controlled horizontal movement.

Dirigibles date back to France in the mid-1850s, but it was in Germany that the idea was perfected, mainly under the guidance and direction of the German businessman Count Ferdinand von Zeppelin. German dominance of the airship industry became so pronounced that the common-usage 'dirigibles' and 'airship' were largely replaced by the term 'zeppelin' to describe all such machines.

During World War I, Germany used hydrogen-filled zeppelins as observation platforms and for dropping bombs on enemy territory, including numerous raids against London. The comparatively slow speed of these machines, combined with their highly inflammable gas envelope, made them easy targets for anti aircraft guns and defending fighter aircraft, and their use was discontinued after 53 of about 70 in the German Naval Airship Division were lost.

After the war, Germany continued with its zeppelin-building, this time aiming at the transatlantic passenger market with the construction of the massive and luxuriously appointed *Graf Zeppelin*. This airship competed against the ocean liners sailing between Europe and America from 1928 to 1937, cutting travelling time virtually in half, and was a highly successful venture.

The *Graf Zeppelin's* success led to the decision to build an even bigger craft—this one was of colossal proportions, at just over 245 metres in length and 41 metres in diameter and able to hold a vast 205 000 cubic metres of gas. The designers intended to use helium, which is less flammable than the highly volatile hydrogen, but America, the main source of the world's helium at the time, refused to supply it, being suspicious of a military motive behind the German request. Four Mercedes-Benz engines powered the monster craft through the air at 137 kilometres an hour, and passengers were treated to luxurious accommodation with panoramic views. This behemoth of the sky, called the *Hindenburg*, redefined the concept of transatlantic travel.

Launched on 4 March 1936, the airship was only a little smaller than the *Titanic*, and remains the largest object ever to have flown. It began commercial flights soon afterwards, travelling between Germany, New York and Rio de Janeiro for the rest of the year, offering passengers five-star comfort and service never before contemplated on an aircraft.

On 3 May 1937, the *Hindenburg* left Frankfurt bound for New York City, carrying ninety-seven passengers and crew, arriving overhead mid-morning on 6 May after an uneventful flight. After a long hold-up because of bad weather, the captain finally decided to attempt a docking with the mooring mast at Lakehurst Field, and slowly nosed the giant machine in close.

Abruptly, and for no apparent reason, the whole airship burst into flames, a giant fireball engulfing its entire length within a matter of seconds. The entire monstrous construction, blazing fiercely, slowly collapsed to the ground and was totally destroyed in a matter of minutes. Miraculously, sixty-two of the people on board escaped the conflagration by leaping through side windows and sprinting clear of the flames.

The reason behind the disaster has never been established beyond doubt, but static electricity is considered the likely culprit, triggering a spark that ignited either the hydrogen, or the flammable outer skin of the zeppelin.

The Jet Engine Takes Off

From the time the Wright Brothers flew into history in the first heavier-than-air machine in 1903, it had been generally assumed that the only way to power all such aircraft was by a propeller which 'gripped' the air in much the same way that a ship's propeller thrusts a ship through water.

At least two men thought differently, however, and their invention was to totally revolutionise the path of powered flight in the latter half of the twentieth century.

Frank Whittle, an Englishman, was an engineer and test pilot with the Royal Air Force, and Hans von Ohain, a German, was an aircraft designer. Working during the same period in the 1930s, but entirely independently of each other, they almost simultaneously invented the jet engine—one of the milestones of aviation history.

Their ideas were virtually identical. Instead of a propeller 'pulling' an aircraft along by rotation through the air, their new engine would thrust the machine forward by expelling high-speed gases from the rear.

While the theory seemed straightforward, the technical difficulties involved were considerable. To make it work, air had to be drawn into a compressor and raised to a high pressure before entering a combustion chamber. Here it was to be mixed with a fuel (such as kerosene) and ignited, thereby raising the temperature of the air, which would then rush through a turbine, some of it being diverted to power the compressor. The rest would exit the engine in a high-velocity 'jet' that produced the thrust required for forward propulsion.

Because these physical processes involved high temperatures and high pressures, the engine components had to be extremely robust, and many early experiments failed because of component fracture.

Nonetheless, the early work of Whittle and von Ohain suggested that there could well be major advantages with the engine, particularly in speed and acceleration, where theory pointed to a vastly improved performance compared to the conventional propeller engine.

Whittle tried in vain to obtain official support for his project. Working largely on his own, he succeeded in taking out a patent for his 'turbojet' engine in 1930. He constructed a 'bench test' engine in 1937, which was developed into an operational unit used to power a Gloster aircraft into flight on 15 May 1941, in the darkest days of World War II.

Von Ohain was more successful in enlisting assistance, receiving support for his research first from the University of Göttingen, and later from the Heinkel aircraft company. He took out a patent on his engine design in 1934, and an operational model was used in the world's first jet-powered aircraft flight on 27 August 1939.

Both the British and German hierarchies seemed slow to realise the potential of the engine for military purposes, although the Germans succeeded in producing the first operational jet fighter, the Messerschmitt 262, late in World War II, but too late to have a telling impact.

In the years after the war, however, the jet engine gradually took over from the propeller engine in much of military and civil aviation, and is now the basic power plant for nearly all the large passenger-carrying aircraft of the world. Dr Hans von Ohain and Sir Frank Whittle are recognised as the co-inventors. After working in isolation for so many years, the two men eventually met after the war.

Whittle died in 1996, and von Ohain in 1998, both honoured as pioneers of twentieth century aviation.

Instead of a propeller 'pulling' an aircraft along by rotation through the air, their new engine would thrust the machine forward by expelling high-speed gases from the rear.

American technicians working on an early jet engine, August 1945.

Nationalist Chinese refugees being sprayed with DDT before being admitted into Taiwan.

DDT Used as an Insecticide

The now-infamous compound DDT has perhaps one of the strangest stories in the history of chemistry, first acclaimed as one of the saviours of humanity, soon afterwards reviled as one of the greatest villains of environmental pollution.

DDT is one of a class of chemicals known as chlorinated hydrocarbons. It was first observed in the laboratory as far back as 1874 by a German chemist called Othmar Zeidler, but no real use for the strange compound was anticipated at the time. Its chemical name is long and complicated and of the form so beloved by organic chemists—dichloro-diphenyl-trichloroethane—which, not surprisingly was abbreviated to DDT.

In 1939 a spectacular use for DDT was discovered when Swiss chemist Paul Mueller demonstrated that it was fabulously successful as an insecticide, even at low rates of application. It was immediately put into action against one of humanity's oldest enemies—the mosquito. Various species of mosquito are responsible for carrying several deadly diseases, among them malaria, encephalitis, yellow fever and dengue fever—and DDT worked against all of those species. The medical profession rejoiced at the possibility of an all-out assault on this primary insect pest. Immediately there were wonderful results, with such a significant drop in malaria over all regions where DDT was used, for example, that it was considered possible that this scourge of humanity might finally be eliminated.

DDT was also found to be highly effective in controlling insect pests in general agriculture. So great was its potential that Paul Mueller was awarded the Nobel Prize in Medicine in 1948 for discovering its application as an insecticide.

But DDT has worrying properties as well. It is virtually insoluble in water—meaning that it does not dissolve and become less concentrated if water is added to it. This in turn means that DDT residues tend to accumulate in the environment, rather than become increasingly diluted as happens with many other chemicals. It does, however, dissolve in oil and fats, and as animals at the lower end of the food chain are eaten by those higher up, the concentration increases, until the highest dose is consumed at the top end of the chain.

This disturbing property was observed to have serious effects on the breeding habits of various high-end avian predators such as cormorants, falcons and eagles, which seemed to produce thinner shells around their eggs, with higher rates of infertility, after exposure to DDT. It was also highly toxic to many fish, even at very low concentrations.

Increasingly worrisome reports about the toxicity of DDT began circulating in the scientific community during the 1950s, but the general public became stunningly aware of the problem through a landmark book published in 1962—*Silent Spring*, by the US biologist and writer Rachel Carson. In it Carson catalogued the environmental disasters that could result from the misuse of synthetic pesticides, such as DDT, with the harm they caused far outstripping any benefits produced.

The publication caused an instant uproar, with chemical companies and even sections of the US government condemning the book as alarmist. But the facts were incontrovertible, and *Silent Spring* produced such an impact that Carson has been credited, single-handedly, with launching the environmental movement that has achieved such prominence today.

DDT was withdrawn from use as an insecticide in most Western countries during the late 1960s and early 1970s. However some critics maintain that the increase in malaria noted since the banning of DDT has produced far worse effects than the use of the chemical itself.

The youthful British air force responded magnificently, and increasingly mauled the German squadrons in savage 'dog-fights' over the English countryside.

Spitfire pilots waiting for the order to 'scramble' during the Battle of Britain, August 1940.

The Battle of Britain

In June 1940, only a few months after the beginning of World War II, the outlook for England appeared particularly bleak. The British army had been defeated in France, although miraculously evacuated by sea from Dunkirk with a minimum of further losses. France had surrendered, and German forces were massing along the beaches of France with only the narrow ribbon of the Channel between them and an England reeling from the recent defeats.

On 18 June 1940, the Prime Minister of Britain, Winston Churchill, informed the House of Commons:

> ... the Battle of France is over. The Battle of Britain is about to begin. Upon this battle depends the survival of Christian civilization, upon it depends our own British life and the long continuity of our institution and our Empire.

He spoke at a juncture when Hitler had ordered a plan to be drawn up for the seaborne invasion of England, earmarked for September 1940. Germany believed that the British Army would not by then have recovered from the debacle in France. The code name for the German invasion was Operation Sea Lion.

The Germans were confident of being able to outgun the Royal Navy provided they had air superiority, so the first stage of the invasion was to be the disabling of the Royal Air Force (RAF)—an operation that the Germans were also confident of achieving.

At that time the German Air Force—the Luftwaffe—was considerably larger than the RAF in both numbers of aircraft and pilots, with many of the British aircrew in particular very young (under twenty years of age) and inexperienced in battle. But the RAF was also equipped with two superb fighters, the Hurricane and Spitfire, both having similar performance to the frontline German Messerschmitt fighters.

Another important factor on the British side was radar. Although only in a primitive early stage of development, this electronic device enabled the RAF's Fighter Command to detect incoming German aircraft well before they arrived over England, and to deploy their own fighters to maximum advantage.

All-out bombing and fighter attacks began over England in August 1940, with the Germans mounting massive air raids against RAF airfields in an attempt to knock out resistance. But the youthful British air force responded magnificently, and increasingly mauled the German squadrons in savage 'dog-fights' over the English countryside. The sky was criss-crossed with white contrails as the airmen of England and Germany fought and killed each other high above the earth in the first major battle in history to be fought entirely in the air.

The conflict continued on a daily basis during September and October, with German casualties steadily mounting, and the RAF, supposedly incapable of effectively resisting the Luftwaffe, fighting with a sustained fury that was steadily tipping the odds towards the British.

By the end of October, Germany was forced to break off the onslaught. Large-scale daylight bombing raids on England largely ceased, ending the period that later became known as the 'Battle of Britain'. Although only a small battle within a much larger war, it must rate as one of the finest victories in the history of British arms.

The Bombing of Pearl Harbor

By mid-1941, World War II had been in progress for nearly two years, with Britain, Russia and their allies locked in mortal combat with the Nazi war machine. The United States, while maintaining an uneasy neutrality, nevertheless stationed a large fleet of warships in the Pacific, with a major naval base strategically located at Pearl Harbor on the island of Oahu in Hawaii.

During the previous decade Japan had been gradually increasing its influence across the Pacific, attacking and occupying parts of China in 1937 with the justification that Japan was the true leader of Asia; Japan also maintained that the Western presence in the region should be swept aside in the interests of all Asian nations.

The United States clearly stood in the way of this ambition, but Japan knew that an open and declared war against America would be highly risky, with no guarantee of success. So an undeclared war was planned, with a paralysing hit on the US naval base at Pearl Harbor the linchpin of the strategy. If the US Pacific Fleet could be heavily damaged or even destroyed in one grand surprise raid, it would be months before the Americans could regain their poise, and by that time Japan would be in a winning position.

A top-secret mission was mounted. On 7 December 1941, Vice-Admiral Chuichi Nagumo was in command of an attack force of 33 ships, including six aircraft carriers, located about 370 kilometres to the north of Pearl Harbor. A mixed force of over four hundred aircraft was aboard the carriers, including fighters, conventional bombers and torpedo-bombers. The latter carried specially designed torpedoes equipped with wooden fins that would allow them to run in the shallow waters of Pearl Harbor—a capability that the Americans considered impossible.

The first wave of aircraft took off around 6 am and headed south, completely unsuspected by the sleeping American naval forces. Just after 7 am the attack formation was picked up by US radar on the north shore of Oahu, but was disregarded as it was believed to be a flight of incoming US B-17 bombers, expected later in the morning. Soon afterwards, a second wave of attack aircraft was launched and headed off towards Pearl Harbor, about 75 minutes behind the first wave.

The Japanese attacked just before 8 am, simultaneously bombing the ships and harbour installations from high levels, strafing the nearby airfield with Zero fighters, and launching the wooden-finned torpedoes from low-flying Kate torpedo-bombers. The results were truly devastating.

Many bombs and torpedoes found their marks, with huge explosions tearing across the harbour, and gigantic columns of smoke darkening the sky. Eight battleships were seriously hit, with five damaged beyond repair. A major casualty was the battleship *USS Arizona*, destroyed by a massive blast triggered by a bomb hitting the ammunition magazine. Over two thousand American sailors lost their lives in the raid, nearly half of them on the Arizona alone.

From Japan's standpoint the raid was initially a massive success, although it did not achieve its aim of totally destroying the Pacific Fleet. But in truth it was a miscalculation on Japan's part, for it was instrumental in bringing the United States into the war, thereby sowing the seeds for the defeat of Japan some four years later. Soon after the attack, Japan's Admiral Yamamoto remarked, 'I fear that all we have done is awaken a sleeping giant and fill him with a terrible resolve.'

Russian tanks on their way to the front on railway carriages.

A blazing Russian T-34 tank during the Battle of Kursk.

A Kamikaze pilot dons a ceremonial head scarf before beginning his mission.

The Rise of the Kamikaze

From mid-1942, the fortunes of the war in the Pacific swung away from the Japanese, despite stunning successes soon after Pearl Harbor in December 1941.

Japan had been heavily defeated in the naval battle of Midway in June 1942, and Allied forces, backed by the massive firepower of the United States, were 'island-hopping' across the Pacific, moving slowly but steadily towards Japan.

The Japanese resistance weakened under the escalating onslaught, with the supply of experienced pilots in particular dwindling to merely a trickle. Without an effective air force, stopping or even slowing down the advancing enemy would be virtually impossible.

A solution to the problem was found which utilised characteristics peculiar to the Japanese culture of the war years, and resulted in an elite, devastating attack force that inflicted heavy damage on the Allies for a comparatively small investment in Japanese lives and equipment.

A special force of volunteers was assembled—mostly trainee pilots who knew the basics of flying but possessed little or no combat experience. Their task was simple. It was to fly an aircraft packed with explosives into Allied shipping, preferably aircraft carriers, with the intention of inflicting as much damage as possible. If a vulnerable area on the target ship was struck in this way it was possible for one aircraft to sink even a major navy vessel. This plan had the potential to turn the war back in favour of Japan. It also, however, meant the certain death of the pilot.

These volunteers were the much-revered Kamikaze, from a word meaning 'divine wind', referring to an event which occurred in 1281, when the naval fleet of the Kublai Khan was smashed by a typhoon when attempting to invade Japan. An overwhelming number of men

An overwhelming number of men volunteered for the Kamikaze, despite each man knowing that his flight would in fact be a suicide mission.

volunteered for the Kamikaze, despite each man knowing that his flight would in fact be a suicide mission. But it was a significant honour to be accepted into this group, for it brought great prestige to the pilot's family and their ancestors, and marked the pilot as a worthy son of *bushido*, the 'warrior spirit'.

The first major success for the Kamikaze occurred on 25 October 1944 when a pilot crashed his aircraft into the deck of the aircraft carrier *USS St Lo*, causing a series of explosions that destroyed the vessel. Increasing numbers of kamikaze attacks were launched from that time, with the force expanding to over two thousand aircraft, comprising a particularly lethal battle group.

The Kamikaze employed two main types of attack. The first was from high altitude, with the pilot selecting a ship, if possible an aircraft carrier, and diving vertically at high speed towards the deck. The other method involved taking a very low flight path, with the plane flying at full throttle just above the sea and slamming into the side or superstructure of the target. The defending vessels would put up a fusillade of anti-aircraft fire, but often the kamikaze pilot was able to penetrate this, and reach the target.

The Kamikaze became a much-feared fighting force, and by 1945, for the loss of around 4000 pilots, they had sunk over eighty ships, and seriously damaged nearly two hundred more. In military terms this could hardly be deemed an efficient use of resources. The Kamikaze's importance lay more in the type of resistance they symbolised—both to Japan and the Allies—the determination to fight to the death.

A V-1 flying bomb being readied for launch during 1944.

A V-1 that crashed in an English field without exploding.

Hitler's Vengeance: the V-1 and V-2 Flying Bombs

By June 1944 the German armies were clearly being defeated on all fronts. British and American forces had successfully landed in France on 6 June, and Russian forces were steamrolling towards Berlin at frightening speed. However, Hitler had one last, terrifying card to play—what he called Vergeltungswaffen, or 'vengeance weapons'.

At that time Germany was ten or fifteen years ahead of the rest of the world in the area of rocket science, largely because of the work of the eminent scientist Wernher von Braun, who would later play a leading role in the development of the American Space Project.

Earlier in the war von Braun and his colleagues had developed perhaps the world's first 'flying bomb', the Vergeltungswaffen 1 or V-1. After much testing and refinement it was finally unleashed against London on 13 June 1944.

The V-1 (nicknamed the 'doodlebug' by the British) was an unmanned aircraft packed with some 830 kilograms of amatol explosive. It had wings and tailfins, and was powered by a type of engine called a 'pulsejet' that produced a sound not unlike a motorbike as it raced across the sky. It could travel at about 645 kilometres an hour over a range of some 240 kilometres, which meant that it could be launched from across the English Channel and used against southern England, in particular, London. The V-1 carried only enough fuel to take it to the target, after which the engine cut out, and it would plunge to earth, creating a huge explosion.

Hundreds were launched at London during the latter half of 1944, killing an estimated six thousand people, although many were shot down by anti-aircraft fire or intercepted by fighter aircraft before they could reach their target.

An even more terrifying and destructive weapon was the Vergeltungswaffen 2 or V-2, a true rocket that could carry nearly 920 kilograms of high explosive over 290 kilometres in a sub-orbital flight before descending nearly vertically on its target at a supersonic speed of around 4800 kilometres an hour.

The first of these rockets was launched at London in September 1944, with over a thousand more fired before the Allies finally knocked out their launch-sites and manufacturing facilities. The destructive power of these weapons was enormous, with a direct hit from a V-2 capable of levelling an entire block of terrace housing in one tremendous explosion.

The destructive power of these weapons was enormous, with a direct hit from a V-2 capable of levelling an entire block of terrace housing in one tremendous explosion.

Unlike the V-1, with its comparatively slow speed and horizontal flight, there was absolutely no defence against the V-2. Its huge velocity and near-vertical trajectory meant there was almost no possibility of a hit from anti-aircraft fire or interception by a fighter plane. Its tremendous descent speed made it virtually invisible, and because it was travelling far faster than the speed of sound there was no audible warning of its approach. People killed by a V-2 would never have heard it coming, for the sound of its approach lagged far behind the rocket itself.

Hitler's V-2s were estimated to have killed around 2500 people, and the fearsome potential of these futuristic weapons produced considerable disquiet among the British population and the government.

The Bombing of Dresden

By February 1945 Nazi Germany was in full retreat with the Allies closing in from all directions and the greatly weakened German Air Force (Luftwaffe) unable to effectively protect German cities from massive bombing raids being mounted by the British and American air forces.

These air raids were becoming more frequent and extensive as the Allies grew stronger and the British philosophy of mass bombing to weaken civilian morale was increasingly employed. There was also a groundswell of British public opinion that demanded revenge be taken on the Germans—revenge for the bombing of southern England, particularly London, earlier in the war, and the blitz of V-1 and V-2 attacks during 1944.

British Air Marshal Arthur Harris was a strong believer in the mass bombing campaign as a way of shortening the war and thereby saving British lives. He was later to note in his memoirs: 'For one thing, it saved the youth of this country and of our allies from being mown down by the military as it was in the war of 1914–1918'.

On 13 February 1945, Harris ordered a huge aerial attack on the ancient city of Dresden, involving a force of nearly eight hundred Lancaster bombers, to be followed up by American raids over the following two days.

The motivation behind the choice of Dresden has been hotly debated ever since. Up until that time it had not been bombed, and according to the Germans had no strategic or military significance. In addition, the population of the city, normally around 650 000 people, had been greatly increased by a flood of refugees fleeing the advancing Soviet forces.

According to the British, however, Dresden was an important communication centre, making it a justifiable military target. There was also the thought that a heavy raid would be an example to the oncoming Russians of the strength of the British and American air forces.

> Thousands of these bombs were dropped directly over the city centre, starting massive blazes that produced gigantic updraughts rising thousands of feet into the air.

The British attacked on schedule, using incendiary bombs designed to create firestorms across the city. Thousands of these bombs were dropped directly over the city centre, starting massive blazes that produced gigantic updraughts rising thousands of feet into the air. Air rushed in from all sides to replace the air carried aloft, creating storm-force winds that sucked people, houses and automobiles into the maelstrom. There were also numerous reports of people on the ground near the fires collapsing and dying due to lack of oxygen, which had all been consumed by the monstrous flames.

In apocalyptic scenes of carnage, about 75 per cent of the city was destroyed and some 35 000 people killed; some modern German estimates place this figure much higher, at around 100 000.

British aircrews were shaken by seeing the ocean of flames raging beneath them, and many began to question the morality of such total warfare. The British Prime Minister, Winston Churchill, a strong advocate of the bombing campaign, was also shaken, and later sent a memorandum to Harris that stated in part:

> It seems to me that the moment has come when the question of bombing of German cities simply for the sake of increasing the terror, should be reviewed. Otherwise we shall come into control of an utterly ruined land.

The destruction of Dresden remains the subject of intense debate to this day, with many modern Germans claiming it to be a war crime.

The ruins of Dresden after the monster raid of February 1945.

The deadly atomic blast over Hiroshima on 6 August 1945.

The Crash of the Comet

Shortly after the end of World War II, it was realised that the future of aviation would largely be driven by the jet engine, and most builders of commercial aircraft began redesigning in line with this change in technology.

The British manufacturer De Havilland was one of the first off the mark, beginning design work on a jet airliner in 1946, with the intention of having a fully operational aircraft ready for service by the early 1950s.

De Havilland constructed the revolutionary Comet, the first commercial passenger-carrying jet aircraft. It had a crew of four, could carry up to 44 passengers and, most significantly, was powered by four De Havilland Ghost turbojet engines. By modern standards the Comet was underpowered for an aircraft of its considerable size, but the new engine technology gave it a performance far in advance of the propeller-driven airliners of the time. It could climb to 12 000 metres, had a range of around 2400 kilometres and could cruise at 725 kilometres an hour, which cut the average time taken for an international journey by as much as half.

The first passenger flight took place in May 1952 between London and Johannesburg, the aircraft creating a sensation with its futuristic looks and high speeds. The jet age had truly arrived in commercial aviation, and the Comet was so successful initially that orders for more than fifty were received from around the world.

Soon afterwards a series of catastrophic crashes sharply decreased public confidence in the aircraft. Late in 1952, and again in early 1953 Comets crashed soon after take-off. Investigation revealed that the wing design produced a sharp drop in lift if the aircraft tried to climb too sharply in the early stages of the flight.

This was followed by two appalling crashes in 1954, with the aircraft suddenly, and without warning, exploding at high altitude, killing everyone aboard. After this the Comet was grounded while further intensive testing was conducted to solve the mystery.

In one of the most intensive episodes of detective work ever carried out in the aviation industry, engineers performed numerous detailed flight tests while monitoring all sections of the aircraft, including the engines. No fault could be found. Then underwater stress tests were conducted, with a Comet fuselage immersed in a water tank to simulate large pressure differences between the inside and outside.

An amazing story emerged. The underwater tests revealed that the metal surrounding the Comet's large rectangular windows began to crack under varying pressure conditions, in a phenomenon known as metal fatigue. The fact that the windows were rectangular produced stress points at the corners. It was believed that these areas failed after repeated flights and the pressure variations associated with climbs and descents. This resulted in the windows shattering. If this occurred at high altitude, explosive decompression would follow, with the aircraft literally tearing itself apart in flight.

There were no further commercial Comet flights until 1958, when the Comet 4 was introduced, a heavily redesigned and more powerful aircraft with one of the main modifications being rounded windows to solve the metal fatigue problem.

The Comet 4 operated successfully around the world until they were gradually phased out of airline fleets in the 1960s, although several individual craft flew until later dates.

> The Comet was so successful initially that orders for more than fifty were received from around the world.

Visibility across the city dropped to less than 50 metres, and all rail, road and air transport ground to a halt.

Visibility was cut to 50 metres across parts of London on 5 December 1952.

Heavenly Creatures

The Parker-Hulme murder was an extraordinary event that shook conservative 1950s New Zealand society to its core and several decades later still reverberates.

In 1954, 16-year-old Pauline Parker and 15-year-old Juliet Hulme were outwardly normal Christchurch schoolgirls. They came from very different backgrounds and were quite dissimilar in personality, Hulme being outgoing, bright and vivacious, Parker more introspective and uncommunicative.

The girls became firm friends and developed a fantasy world in which they became completely convinced that they would write a series of novels that would later be made into films in Hollywood. Often, at night, they would act out characters from these novels. They also developed their own religion, believing that they were superior to other people and held a special status in the universe. In a poem Parker wrote for Hulme, she described them both as 'goddesses' that 'reign on high', and as 'heavenly creatures'.

Their parents, initially happy that the girls had become such good friends, became increasingly concerned that the relationship was going beyond normal schoolgirl boundaries, and decided to end it by separating them. Hulme's father planned to relocate his family to South Africa. When Parker asked if she could go with them, her mother, Honora, refused. The girls were determined not to be separated, however.

On 22 June 1954, they invited Honora to walk with them in Christchurch's vast Victoria Park. As they strolled down a lonely track, Parker produced a half brick held in a stocking and swung it at her mother's head. She repeatedly bashed her mother with the brick, assisted by Hulme, who also landed several hits. Honora died of multiple contusions caused by some forty-five blows to the head in the frenzied attack.

> Parker produced a half brick held in a stocking and swung it at her mother's head.

The girls claimed that Honora Parker had fallen and hit her head, but the police soon dismissed that possibility and the two girls were arrested and charged with murder. The background to the killing was revealed to a horrified New Zealand public in the sensational court case that followed.

Defence counsel tried to argue that the girls were not guilty by reason of insanity, but this assertion was vigorously rebutted by the prosecution. One medical witness was of the opinion that the girls knew murder was wrong but, because they were 'special', they considered that the normal rules of society did not apply to them. Hints of lesbianism also surfaced—this was discussed in the newspapers as an example of how non-mainstream relationships led to perversions and anti-social behaviour, a point of view which fitted in neatly with the social mores of the day. The Crown Prosecutor remarked in his summing up to the jury: 'This was a coldly, callously planned and carefully committed murder by two precocious and dirty-minded little girls. They are not incurably insane, but incurably bad.'

Parker and Hulme were both found guilty of murder in August of 1954, and sentenced to be detained at 'Her Majesty's pleasure'. They were released in 1959 on the strict condition that they would never again contact each other.

In 1994, New Zealand film director Peter Jackson released a film about the incident called *Heavenly Creatures*, starring Melanie Lynskey and Kate Winslet. The interest created by the film led both Parker and Hulme, then in their fifties, to live separately in Britain under changed names.

Alarm bells began to ring in the early 1950s, when suspicions were raised about the possible link between smoking and lung cancer.

In 1954 a scientific paper was published establishing a strong statistical connection between smoking and lung cancer.

The Plastic Bag

Plastics, or their derivatives, date back at least to the 1860s, when several experimenters produced polymer products by combining cellulose with coal tar in various proportions. But it was the Belgian chemist Leo Baekland who took the quantum leap forward in 1907, when he developed the first fully synthetic plastic by mixing phenol with formaldehyde.

The resulting substance was named Bakelite, and was found to be a tough, durable, waterproof material ideal for a wide variety of industrial and domestic purposes. Baekland was also credited with inventing the word 'plastic', derived from a Greek word meaning 'to form'.

An increasing variety of plastics appeared as chemists experimented with this fascinating new substance. There seemed to be no limit to the uses and ways in which it could be employed. Telephones, radio cabinets, billiard balls, buttons, toilet seats, table tops, fans, automobile parts and space suits could all be made from plastic, and as the twentieth century progressed plastic became synonymous with the modern age.

It was also found that bags made of plastic could be manufactured. Strong, hygienic, feather-light and moisture-proof, they were the perfect packaging device for school lunches, loaves of bread, clothes storage and garbage disposal.

In 1957 the first plastic bag roll was produced, making for an easy and convenient dispensing method, and over the next four decades plastic bags became ever more ubiquitous. In particular, they became immensely popular as grocery bags, with most of the big supermarket chains adopting them as standard for packing customers' groceries at the checkout. These bags were widely re-used as garbage receptacles, and dumped at local garbage tips through suburban waste collection systems. By 1996 it was estimated that four out of five grocery bags in the Western world were made of plastic.

Then it became obvious that a problem was emerging. Tens of millions of bags were accumulating in the environment, both on land and in the oceans, with sailors reporting that the most common man-made object seen on the seas of the world was the plastic bag. This situation was lethal to many marine animals, with ingestion of plastic bags killing many thousands of whales, dolphins, turtles, pelicans and seals each year.

On land the plastic bag became a major item of pollution, littering streets and blocking drains and gutters, often leading to flash flooding in heavy rain situations. In fact, the blocking of drains by plastic bags was believed to be a major factor in the floods across Bangladesh in 1998.

Durability, originally one of the main points of attraction of plastic bags, quickly became one of the main drawbacks. Some estimations in the 1990s pointed to a 'bag life' of up to a thousand years, meaning that unless quick action was taken their rapid accumulation across the world's ecosystems was a recipe for disaster.

Ireland reacted early by imposing a tax on the use of plastic shopping bags in 2002. This was highly effective, resulting in a 90 per cent reduction in their usage in just six months. Many other countries have followed the Irish example, or introduced other strategies to discourage high-volume usage, including recycling projects and the use of inexpensive but re-usable shopping bags made of other materials. Science quickly came up with the biodegradable plastic bag, which is fine for waste collection and disposal, but still poses a threat to animal life until it breaks down.

The plastic bag is an interesting example of a technological advance that produces both positive and negative effects.

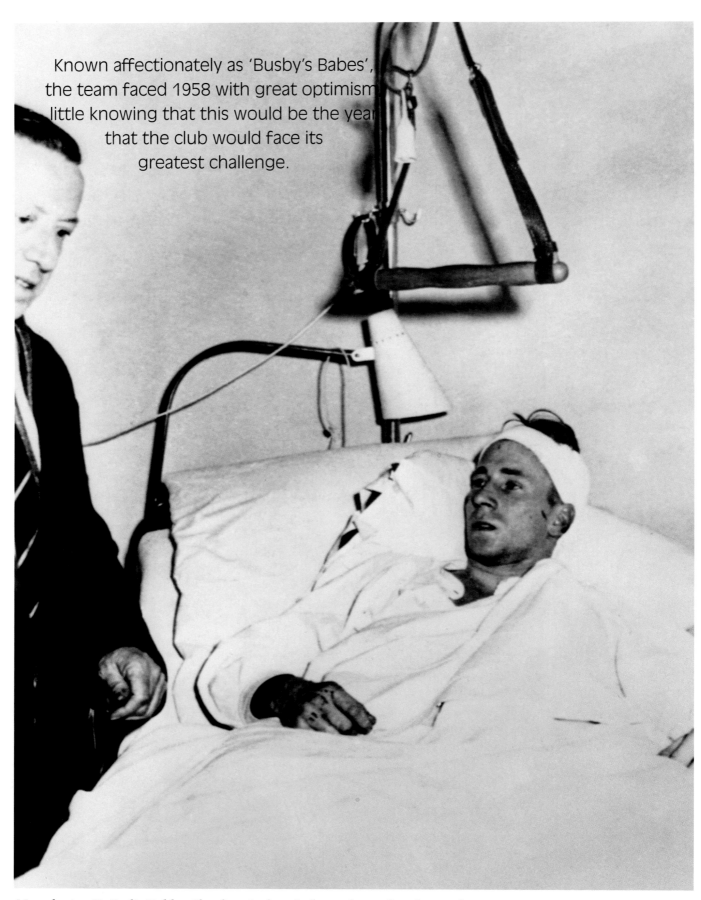

Known affectionately as 'Busby's Babes', the team faced 1958 with great optimism, little knowing that this would be the year that the club would face its greatest challenge.

Manchester United's Bobby Charlton in hospital two days after the crash.

The Lincoln Continental drives through the streets of Dallas.

The motorcade only minutes before the President was shot.

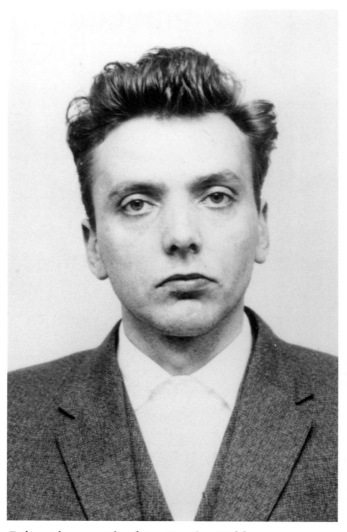
Police photograph of Ian Brady, 1966.

Police photograph of Myra Hindley, 1966.

The mother of victim Lesley Anne Downey watches police search the moors for her daughter's body.

Now with unfettered power, he began a murderous pursuit of all those he distrusted.

President Idi Amin arrives at Gatwick Airport, England, in 1971.

The clash between British troops and protestors led to a massive escalation of 'The Troubles'.

A cyclist wears a face-mask as he passes the Bhopal Union Carbide plant.

About ten minutes
before midnight
a tremendous
explosion shook the
entire vessel, and
both captain and
engineer raced below
to investigate.

The Rainbow Warrior *salvaged at the moorings in Auckland Harbour.*

The *Challenger* Disaster

On the morning of 28 January 1986 a large crowd gathered around the Kennedy Space Centre in Florida to watch the launch of the National Aeronautics and Space Administration (NASA) Space Shuttle *Challenger*, due to embark on its tenth mission into space.

Aboard *Challenger* was a crew of seven, including the commander, Francis Scobee, veteran of a previous shuttle mission, and Christa McAuliffe, the first teacher to fly in a space shuttle, under the recently commissioned Teachers in Space program.

Several technical and weather problems had led to launch delays in the days before, but on this morning there were high expectations that the flight would finally get under way, despite the cold start to the day. Early temperatures were well below average, with frost settling across the area in the early hours and patches of ice actually coating parts of the launch pad.

At 11.38 am, *Challenger* finally lifted off, in what appeared to be a normal launch, and began the rapidly accelerating climb that would take it into an orbital flight high above the earth. Then things began to go wrong.

Ground observers noticed a glowing light on the side of the right solid fuel rocket booster, which was followed only seconds later by what appeared to be a tremendous explosion. Just 73 seconds into the flight a shower of smoke and debris formed a giant plume in the clear skies above, and debris tumbled down in all directions. It was obvious to all that *Challenger* was lost.

For the large crowd on site, which included many friends and relatives of the crew, for the millions watching live on television and for NASA, it was a profoundly shocking event. It dominated the news services around the world for the rest of the day, and was replayed repeatedly on television broadcasts. NASA officials suspended all forthcoming shuttle flights until further notice, and ordered an immediate investigation.

A Presidential Commission on the Space Shuttle *Challenger* Accident was convened, with several very high-profile participants sitting on the committee. These included astronaut Neil Armstrong, famous military pilot Chuck Yeager and eminent physicist Richard Feynman. The accident was dissected in minute detail over a period of several months, and a report assembled for public release.

This report indicated that the direct cause of the disaster was the escape of a jet of high-temperature flame from the right solid fuel rocket booster that played like a blowtorch on the adjacent body of the vehicle. This precipitated a structural failure that exposed the entire vehicle train to the massive aerodynamic forces generated by the rapid acceleration, and the structure was almost instantly torn apart. It was thought that at least some of the crew survived the disintegration, only to die some three or four minutes later when their capsule tumbled from the sky and smashed into the sea.

But the key question was: what had caused the flame leak from the rocket booster in the first place? Feynman was able to produce the answer when he demonstrated that the rubber O-rings that were supposed to form a seal around the boosters were increasingly vulnerable to failure in low temperatures—and the icy conditions before launch time could therefore have been a major factor in the disaster. In fact, it was alleged that NASA management had been aware of serious erosion of the O-rings (short of burn-through) since the start of shuttle flights but had failed to heed the warnings of their own engineers.

As a result of the inquiry, NASA made major changes to the space shuttle program involving several engineering and management practices, which were incorporated into all future missions.

Ben Johnson: Drugs in Sport

On 24 September 1988, the finalists lined up for one of the glamour events of the Seoul, South Korea, Summer Olympics. It was the 100 metres men's track final, with the winner expected to be able to lay legitimate claim to being the fastest runner in the world.

The final was expected to be fought out between the two greatest sprinters of the era, Carl Lewis of the United States and Ben Johnson of Canada, great rivals both on and off the track, a rivalry not always completely friendly.

The starter's gun went, and Johnson exploded off the mark, accelerated smoothly into an upright running stance and simply whizzed away from the field. Just before he crossed the line, well ahead of the other runners, he eased off and glanced back at second-placed Lewis, raising a single finger to indicate that he was now number one. The time was stunning—easily a new world record at 9.79 seconds—and in setting it he also became the first human to break 9.8 seconds for the 100 metres. It was the dream race for Johnson—a world and Olympic record, the gold medal and the unassailable title of 'World's Fastest Human'.

The athletics world rejoiced at the magnitude of the run, and Johnson was proclaimed a national hero in Canada. Canadian Prime Minister Brian Mulroney personally congratulated Johnson by telephone, informing him: 'It's a marvellous evening for Canada'.

But the celebrations were to be short-lived. According to the protocol of the day, Johnson had previously provided a urine sample to an International Olympic Committee (IOC) approved laboratory, and soon after his win this sample was divided into two parts, A and B, for analysis. This was to provide a double check in case the first sample produced some sort of anomalous result. In another procedural safeguard, the identity of the specimen provider was kept secret from the laboratory, and known only to the Chairman of the IOC Medical Commission.

Specimen A was tested and the presence of minute quantities of a banned substance, a type of anabolic steroid, was revealed. The Chairman, aware that the sample came from Johnson, contacted officials in the Canadian team and invited them to attend the testing of the B sample, the result of which would either exonerate or incriminate Johnson. Sample B proved positive as well.

This was catastrophic news, not only for the Canadian Team, but for the Olympic movement in general, still trying to move away from the rampant drug allegations of the Olympic Games of the 1970s involving the Eastern bloc nations. It was always assumed that the West was squeaky clean where drugs in sport were concerned, but the Johnson affair was threatening to totally unravel that theory.

In what was becoming one of the greatest athletics scandals in history, Johnson was stripped of his gold medal, which instead was awarded to the second-placed Carl Lewis, and his world record time was struck from the books. The news was received with great dismay back in Canada, where Johnson's fall from grace was rapid and decisive.

Johnson argued that he had never taken steroids, and if they had been present in his sample it must have been through an act of sabotage. Later, under the stress of repeated questioning, he finally admitted to lying and to being a regular steroid taker before the Olympics. Later on he was to remark: 'I did something good in my life. My mom and dad saw me run faster than any human, and that's it. Better than a gold medal.'

The starter's gun went and Johnson exploded off the mark, accelerated smoothly into an upright running stance and simply whizzed away from the field.

Ben Johnson rocketing down the straight in the Olympic 100 metre final at Seoul, 24 September 1988.

Success followed success, with The Carpenters also becoming one of the most popular international touring acts of the time.

Karen Carpenter in concert: her magical voice entranced the music fans of the 1970s.

Anorexia Nervosa: The Death of Karen Carpenter

During the late 1960s just one kind of music, rock and roll, ruled the airwaves in a manner not seen before or since, and for those a little tired of the endless bump and grind there was little relief on the horizon. Then unexpectedly it came, from a totally unlikely source, out of middle America.

Karen and Richard Carpenter were a brother and sister act that had come about through their family's interest in music. They formed a trio with another artist in 1966, but launched out on their own in 1969, calling themselves simply The Carpenters.

Richard was extremely clever musically, and his vocals formed an airy background to most of their music. However, it was Karen's magical voice that launched the pair to stardom. It was a flawless light contralto, and her melodic interpretations of some of the popular music of the day remain the yardstick by which ballads are judged up to the present time.

Their first album was called *Offering*, followed by the single 'Close to You', which reached Number One in several countries. This was the beginning of a sensational run of Top Twenty singles that propelled The Carpenters to international stardom.

Richard revealed his genius for music selection when he noticed an obscure Californian bank television commercial showing a newlywed couple about to embark on their life together, backed with a melody written by the song-writing team of Paul Williams and Roger Nichols. The Carpenters' remake of this song, called 'We've Only Just Begun', was not only a worldwide smash hit but also became the anthem for many newlyweds of the 1970s.

Success followed success, with The Carpenters also becoming one of the most popular international touring acts of the time. Several of their songs were among the bestsellers of the era, including 'Top of the World', 'Rainy Days and Mondays', 'Yesterday Once More' and 'A Kind of Hush'. The Carpenters had become the first choice of those weary of the endless rock and roll fare served up by the music industry. With millions of records sold and legions of adoring fans, their life had become a fairytale success story.

But behind the glitz and glamour, all was not well. Karen had slowly but inexorably fallen into the grip of what was then the little-publicised psychological condition of anorexia nervosa. Apparently playfully called 'chubby' in her earlier years, she became obsessed with keeping her weight down, even though she had a naturally slender physique; illogically, she starved herself for extended periods.

Her face became noticeably gaunt during the mid 1970s and although she was able to hide her emaciated body from the public to a certain extent by clever choice of clothes, her family was aware of the situation and became frantic with worry.

She collapsed on stage in 1975, and after being rushed to hospital was found to be nearly 16 kilograms underweight. Visits to doctors and therapists followed and for a time it appeared as though she was cured. Sadly, however, her body had been chronically weakened by the years of starvation, and she died of a heart attack in 1983 at the age of only thirty-two.

Her death had the immediate effect of raising public awareness of the seldom-mentioned condition of anorexia nervosa, with thousands then seeking treatment for the elusive disease.

The village of Lockerbie the day after the disaster.

Lockerbie

On 21 December 1988, Pan American Flight 103 took off from Heathrow Airport in London on a trans-Atlantic flight to New York. Aboard were 234 passengers and sixteen crew, some probably mildly irritated with the 25-minute delay caused by the usual congestion at Heathrow. The big 747 climbed away to the north over Scotland, and just over half an hour later reached its cruising level around 9450 metres.

Air traffic controllers monitoring the flight watched the small radar blip as it crept across the screen—but just before three minutes past 7 pm, some 37 minutes after takeoff, it suddenly disappeared.

Around the same time the residents of the small Scottish town of Lockerbie were settling down to a cosy winter's evening when they were startled by a blinding flash in the sky above, followed by a thunderous detonation. Then the sky was filled with glowing embers, raining downwards 'like meteors'. Wreckage began to fall among the houses, with burning fuel also raining down, setting fire to everything it touched. It became horribly apparent that a large aircraft had disintegrated above the town.

A huge chunk of metal, later shown to be a major part of the wing assembly loaded with fuel, hurtled into the ground near the southern part of Lockerbie and exploded, forming a massive crater. Wreckage continued to fall from the sky, eventually covering an area of some 130 square kilometres. The nose section, including the cockpit, fell virtually intact into a field just a few miles out of town, its windows and windscreen wipers still in place.

It was soon discovered that the aircraft was Pan American Boeing 747 Flight 103, and that all 259 people aboard had been killed, together with eleven residents of Lockerbie. In addition, twenty-one houses in the town had been completely destroyed by fire and impact damage. A massive international investigation was immediately launched.

Forensic testing of the debris soon revealed a chilling scenario. Traces of the military explosive Semtex were found, and investigators concluded that a concealed bomb with a timing device had been placed aboard the luggage compartment prior to departure. If the flight had been running on time, rather than twenty-five minutes late, the aircraft would have exploded over the ocean rather than above Lockerbie, and evidence would have been almost impossible to find.

Investigation led to the suspicion that Libya was behind the disaster, perhaps as revenge for the US bombing of their country in 1986. The hunt for the perpetrators became focused on two men, Abdelbaset Ali Mohmed al-Megrahi and Al Amin Khalifa Fhimah, both of whom had returned to Libya after the crash. Megrahi was a Libyan intelligence officer, and Fhima the manager of Libyan Arab Airlines operations in Malta, where it was alleged the bomb had originated.

Both the US and UK governments demanded that they be extradited for trial, but the Libyan leader Muammar Qaddafi refused this request. The United Nations then placed economic sanctions on Libya, which remained in place until 1999, when Qaddafi finally agreed to hand both men over for trial in a neutral venue, the Netherlands. Despite continually protesting his innocence, Megrahi was found guilty of murder and sentenced to twenty-seven years in prison. Fhimah was found not guilty and later released.

The disaster was also a devastating blow to Pan American Airlines, and was probably a major factor in the company's demise in 1991.

The *Exxon Valdez* Oil Spill

Late at night on 23 March 1989, the large oil tanker *Exxon Valdez* was picking its way carefully through the waters of Prince William Sound, off the coastline of Alaska. This is essentially a large bay containing many islands and surrounded by a rugged coastline.

Several active glaciers feed into the bay, with chunks of ice continually breaking away and floating off as icebergs of various sizes, the smaller ones being known as 'growlers'. While these are nowhere near the majestic size of classical icebergs, they can be big enough to represent a shipping hazard, and are normally avoided, even by large vessels. There are also areas of shallow water and reefs in Prince William Sound. With all these hazards, large shipping usually follows prescribed channels or lanes to allow the safest passage.

On the bridge of the *Exxon Valdez* that night, Captain Hazelwood radioed the local Coastguard requesting permission to change course in order to avoid a number of growlers from the nearby Columbia Glacier that had drifted across the shipping lanes. Permission received, he retired for the night, leaving the third mate in command, and ordering him to come back to the original course once the ship had reached a certain landmark.

About four minutes past midnight, the ship began turning to the right in an apparent attempt to return to its original course, and in doing so smashed into nearby Blight Reef, tearing open a large section in the hull. The results were catastrophic.

Some 42 million litres of crude oil spilled out into the ocean and began slowly dispersing in a south-westerly direction. Desperate attempts to contain the spill were immediately launched, but all efforts were unable to prevent one of the most disastrous pollution events in history.

Three main techniques were used to remedy the situation, but the remote locality mitigated against getting sufficient equipment to the site quickly enough and unfavourable weather conditions made clean-up attempts difficult to implement. A section of the slick was separated from the main pool and ignited, but the unfavourable weather limited the success of this operation. Then mechanical means were tried, involving attempts to cordon off the spill with floating barriers and 'skim' the oil from the surface, but the equipment available could not handle the vast quantity involved. Finally, chemical dispersants were sprayed from above from a helicopter, but the weather conditions also counted against the effectiveness of this method.

Over the next days and weeks the slick gradually continued to move south-west, past Kodiak Island and down the east coast of the Alaskan Peninsula. Thousands of sea birds were trapped in the slick and died, just part of a massive death toll extending to sea otters, seals, and countless fish of many types.

The aftermath was also massive, with litigation continuing for many years, resulting in punitive damages against the Exxon company awarded to a large number of plaintiffs who claimed that their businesses had been compromised, and claims from indigenous American groups whose livelihoods had also been affected by the disaster. The US Congress also passed the *Oil Pollution Act of 1990*, which included a clause specifically banning the *Exxon Valdez* from Alaskan waters.

Up until this spill occurred there had been a certain public perception that the environmental movement was powered by an extremist anti-industrial philosophy that exaggerated the dangers posed to the environment by modern society. The shocking television images of the oil spill and its consequences changed all this, and there was a considerable raising in awareness of the need to care for our planet and its ecosystems.

Desperate attempts to contain the spill were immediately launched, but all efforts were unable to prevent one of the most disastrous pollution events in history.

Two weeks after the oil spill the Exxon Valdez *is towed off the reef.*

A nurse waits under a hospital banner during the standoff in Tiananmen Square.

Tiananmen Square

Tiananmen Square is an extensive public gathering area in the centre of Beijing in China. The square has particular historical relevance to the Communist Party of China, with Chairman Mao Zedong having proclaimed the founding of the Peoples' Republic of China there in 1949.

Several important public buildings are located around the square, including the Museum of History and Revolution, the Mao Zedong Memorial Hall and the Great Hall of the People. Tiananmen Square is also the site of one of the worst incidents in the history of modern China, where the forces of the Army were turned en masse against unarmed Chinese civilians. Ironically, Tiananmen means 'Gate of Heavenly Peace'.

Demonstrations in favour of democratic reform had slowly gathered momentum during April of 1989, beginning with a few students but ending up involving many thousands of others, including workers, intellectuals and public servants, day after day filling the square with a vast throng.

On 15 May, a much publicised and historic meeting between the Chinese and Russian leaders was planned to take place, part of an extensive State visit by Russian officials. The student leaders of the demonstrations became determined to bring their cause to the attention of the world through the reports that would be filed by the large number of overseas journalists covering the meeting; undoubtedly they also intended to embarrass the Government in front of the Russian officials.

Thousands more protesters converged on the square two days before the meeting, declaring a hunger strike until the Government agreed to see their leaders. Communist Party officials made several attempts over the next few days to persuade the hunger strikers to leave, but they refused.

Abruptly, the Chinese Government decided that enough was enough. Late on 3 June, some seven weeks after the demonstrations had begun, tanks rumbled into Tiananmen Square, backed up by hundreds of troops who converged on the square from several different streets and laneways. The soldiers opened fire, shooting at the protesters at random but with deadly intent nonetheless, causing thousands to flee in panic. Other protesters, assisted by local citizens, rescued countless casualties as they lay and took them to nearby hospitals, but many were already dead.

Two days later, on 5 June, a lone protester, a worker who abandoned his bicycle, stood in front of a line of four advancing tanks, blocking their progress. He stood there for half an hour, defiant, until he was hauled away by onlookers, thought to be other workers. The photograph of this scene became, to the rest of the world, the iconic image of Tiananmen Square, symbolising the rights of the individual against the overwhelming power of the State. Many of the events following the military intervention were broadcast live by Western media present to cover the Russian State visit, but the Chinese Government eventually shut down these communiqués, notably those issuing from the BBC and CNN.

Against the might of the military, the protest was inevitably quashed, but the incident attracted extensive international condemnation, especially from the West. The Chinese Government, severely embarrassed, pushed the line that it had merely put an end to a 'counter-revolutionary rebellion'.

The casualty figures have always been in dispute, as the actual numbers of dead and wounded remain a State secret. Estimates vary from hundreds to well into the thousands, with one claim alleging four thousand dead and 30 000 wounded. It is unlikely the true numbers will ever be known outside China. Discussion of the event within China is officially discouraged and no anniversary ceremonies are permitted.

An anxious, jostling crowd began to build up at the Leppings Lane end of the ground, and police in charge of the situation became increasingly concerned with the mounting crush around the turnstile area.

Rescuers try to pull those below from the crush up against the steel mesh fence.

Hillsborough Soccer Disaster

For both the Liverpool and Nottingham Forest football clubs, 15 April 1989 was set to be an exciting day. The two clubs had reached the FA Cup Semi-Final, to be held at Hillsborough, a neutral ground in Sheffield, England.

At the time the FA (Football Association) had been experiencing considerable trouble with violent incidents between the spectators of opposing clubs, with outbreaks of fighting and rioting sometimes spilling over from the terraces onto the field itself. Crowd control had become a big issue, and strong, open-meshed steel fencing had been erected at several of the main grounds in an attempt to both segregate rival spectators and to prevent the crowd from invading the playing surface.

As the 3 pm kick-off time approached, it was clear there were crowd problems. Heavy traffic congestion had delayed the arrival of many Liverpool fans, large numbers of whom were now attempting to enter the stadium before the match started. An anxious crowd began to build up at the Leppings Lane end of the ground, and police became increasingly concerned with the mounting crush around the turnstile area.

In an effort to improve crowd flow, they ordered another set of gates, which were not impeded by turnstiles, to be opened. Hundreds of fans poured through and forced their way into the ground. While this relieved the pressure outside the stadium, it proved a disaster inside for those closest to the playing area. The game began, but the increasing pressure caused by spectators pushing in from the rear began to force those standing around the boundary up against the heavy steel-mesh fencing erected to keep them off the field.

Police and officials watched in alarm as the crush worsened. The game was stopped as soon as it became apparent that people's lives were actually in danger. Desperate to escape the crush, some fans climbed the fence and jumped over onto the playing area; others were lifted to safety by spectators in the tier above.

But for those trapped against the fence and who could not climb it, the situation was disastrous: people in their hundreds were crushed against the steel mesh or trampled to the ground, unable to move. Some died there against the fence, begging for help from those on the other side, who were literally within touching distance but quite unable to do anything

When the crush finally cleared, the injured, together with the bodies of the dead, were assembled on the field, where shocked police, officials and medical staff attended to them. Soon the enormity of the disaster became apparent— 96 people had died and 766 were injured. An outraged British public demanded to know what happened and why.

An official investigation was convened by Lord Justice Taylor, who eventually produced a report that changed the mechanics and philosophy of crowd control in English soccer venues. Two of the major recommendations were the removal of steel mesh fences from around the grounds, and that seating be provided for all patrons, thereby eliminating the high-density crushes so often found in standing room-only areas.

A well-known British tabloid newspaper later published an account of the disaster which blamed some of the problems on 'drunken Liverpool fans', an allegation officially denied in Lord Taylor's report. Boycotts of the paper were immediately organised throughout the Liverpool region, and to this day that paper's circulation remains substantially reduced in the area.

The Rise of Obesity

One of the eternal problems faced by early humanity was the daily battle to find enough food to survive. Societies slowly progressed from 'hunter–gatherer' to agricultural, until eventually humans moved on to the more reliable food provision methods of the modern industrial society.

It is a supreme irony that one of the major problems to confront twenty-first century Western societies is not a lack of food, but too much of it, with many serious health issues associated with the growing phenomenon of obesity.

A simple, but not universally agreed upon definition of obesity is when the body weight reaches 10 per cent or more than the figure recommended for the height and body type for each sex. And the simple cause of obesity is the eating of more kilojoules than the body is using up or, more simply put—too much food and too little exercise.

Americans in particular are getting bigger. Studies have shown that the average American adult male of today is just 2.5 centimetres taller, but a whopping 11 kilograms heavier than his 1960s counterpart. Similar, although somewhat smaller increases, have emerged in other Western countries over the same time frame.

Governments of many Western nations have become concerned about the increasingly sedentary lifestyles of their citizens, a large amount of whose leisure time is taken by watching television and playing computer games rather than engaging in physical activities such as sport.

The results of a sedentary lifestyle have become particularly obvious in children, whose lack of exercise has been linked with the steadily increasing onset of childhood obesity, with many then taking their condition through to adulthood. The average American ten-year-old is an estimated 5 kilograms heavier than the equivalent child of forty years ago.

The type of food consumed in many countries in the West, not just America, is also a factor, with sectors of the fast food industry often dispensing products high in sugar and fat, as well as targeting children in their advertising strategies. With economic pressures now demanding that both parents in a typical family work, more takeaway food is being purchased because the time to prepare home-cooked meals has proportionately decreased.

A particular worry with obesity is its close association with a number of chronic diseases such as cancer, diabetes, high blood pressure and heart conditions, and medical experts have become increasingly concerned that obesity may soon outstrip tobacco as the leading cause of preventable death in the twenty-first century.

The average life expectancy for humans, particularly those in the developed world, has steadily increased in the last few centuries, due to numerous advances such as reliable sewerage systems, the decrease of infant mortality, progress in medicine, and an increasingly reliable food-providing system. In medieval England, for example, the average life expectancy was only around 33 years, whereas it is now around 77 to 81 years.

The twentieth century in particular saw a dramatic increase in life expectancy across many societies, including India and China, in addition to the West. But some experts are now considering that the threat produced by the modern epidemic of obesity is so serious that the trend to increased life expectancy may be in danger of peaking and even reversing over the next few decades or so.

This alarming prognosis is presenting a major challenge to governments in many countries, and numerous strategies to deal with the situation are now evolving.

The average American ten-year-old is an estimated 5 kilograms heavier than the equivalent child of the 1960s.

Obesity amongst young people is a rising problem right across the western world.

In the early 1990s, a wave of RMS cases, usually involving young women under some form of psychotherapy, grabbed the headlines in the United States.

Repressed memory syndrome became a headline event of the 1990s.

Repressed Memory Syndrome

Repressed memory syndrome (RMS) is the name given to a psychiatric condition in which recollection of a past incident or incidents is subconsciously hidden from the memory, usually because of their painful or traumatic nature. In other words, although the memories are stored away, they cannot be recalled because the individual subconsciously represses them.

This is supposedly a damaging mental condition that can be cured when the individual is finally able to recall the lost memories and face up to the past. Guided by a professional therapist, recollection is usually attempted through hypnosis, drug-mediated interviews or dream interpretation.

RMS is also the cause of tremendous controversy, with many experts doubting that the condition exists at all. The treatment of RMS has precipitated the break-up of many families and led to numerous court cases, mainly in the United States, as alleged victims and perpetrators sought redress.

In the early 1990s, a wave of RMS cases, usually involving young women under some form of psychotherapy, grabbed the headlines in the United States. Past events were recalled, often involving sexual abuse of some form, and often implicating a close family member such as the woman's father. In some of these cases public accusation followed, and the alleged perpetrator was arrested and tried on the basis of the recollections alone. Hundreds of families were ripped apart, and a climate of fear and suspicion was created.

In an early example in 1989, a young woman undergoing hypnosis therapy soon began having vivid and detailed recollections of her father raping and murdering a young friend. The murder had in fact occurred, some twenty years earlier, and was never solved, so police were extremely interested in her story when she reported it. Her father was subsequently tried, found guilty and jailed in what was thought to be the first time an American had been convicted of murder on the basis of RMS.

Lengthy debate about RMS inevitably followed. Sceptics labelled it 'false memory syndrome', arguing that the nature of the therapy itself produced the effect. Under hypnosis in particular, they argued, it was possible for the therapist to 'plant' ideas and suggestions in patients' minds and to 'coach' them through question and answer sessions. Believers countered this argument by noting that sceptics were probably denying their own painful past or were even perpetrators of abuse themselves.

The publication of a book entitled *The Courage to Heal* encouraged people who thought they had been victims of abuse to undergo therapy and come forward. Critics alleged it was a populist work by two authors who had no psychological training, and had merely based their views on personal experience.

In the later 1990s, opinion began to shift heavily against the theory of RMS, as an increasing number of former patients began to come forward and deny their previous allegations of abuse, no longer believing that they had, in fact, been victims. Numerous medical malpractice suits were launched, culminating in a successful multi-million dollar award to an Illinois family in 1997.

Today the attempted recovery of repressed memories through hypnosis or other forms of therapy is an unusual practice and psychiatrists have generally returned to more conventional forms of treatment.

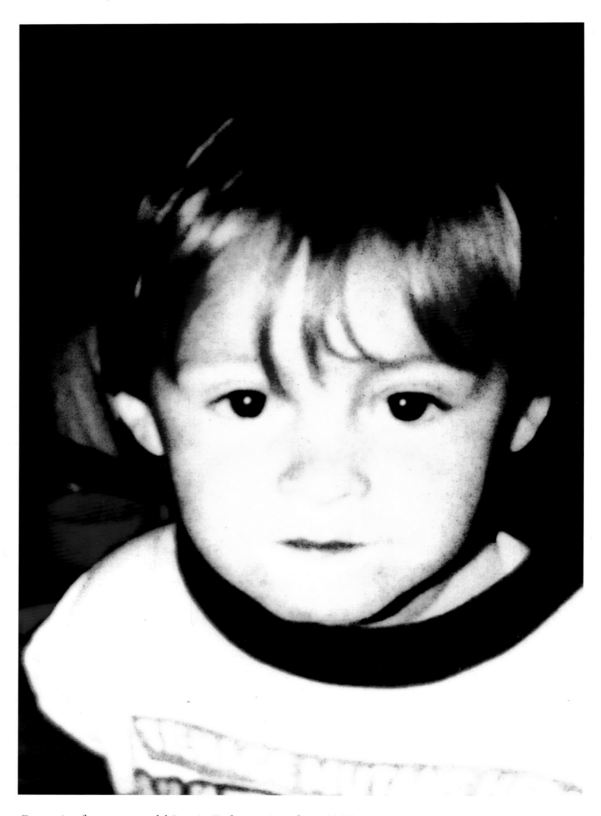

Portrait of two-year-old Jamie Bulger, circa late 1992.

The Death of Jamie Bulger

On 12 February 1993, two ten-year-old boys decided to wag school. They wandered into their neighbourhood shopping centre, the Bootle Strand, at Liverpool in England. Apparently they had conceived the idea of kidnapping a young child, and during the earlier part of the day tried to walk away with a toddler, being foiled when the mother intervened.

Later in the afternoon they succeeded in luring two-year-old Jamie Bulger to them, and led him from the shopping centre, with Jamie's mother for a short time unaware of his disappearance. The closed circuit television system in the shopping centre recorded the scene, and images of Jamie, hand in hand with one of his kidnappers, provided haunting evidence of the beginnings of a crime that was to rock the British nation, and much of the world, as the details were eventually revealed.

The two boys, John Venables and Robert Thompson, came from deprived and dysfunctional families. Venables' parents were separated, his mother suffered from severe depression, and his two siblings experienced significant learning disabilities. Thompson's background was disastrous, with an alcoholic mother and a violent, drunken father who had left the family when Thompson was only five.

Both families lived in one of the poorest parts of Liverpool, itself one of the poorest cities in England at the time. In their young lives Venables and Thompson had learned that the world was a tough place where few people cared and no mercy was shown. By the time they had reached their tenth birthdays, they had completely adopted the same philosophy.

They left the Bootle Strand with Jamie and led him on a long walk towards the local railway line, passing many people on the way, several of whom later recalled these chance encounters. Because there seemed nothing seriously out of the ordinary with the situation, no one intervened, and Jamie was taken to a lonely area of industrial wasteland adjacent to the railway tracks.

Here Venables and Thompson beat, kicked and clubbed the defenceless toddler unconscious, then dragged his limp body to the railway line and placed it prostrate on the tracks, before departing the scene.

In the meantime Jamie's mother had raised the alarm, but no sign of him was found that day or the next. But on the third day a gruesome discovery was made. Jamie's body was found by the railway line, cut in half by a passing train. Immediately suspecting foul play, the police began their investigations.

Venables and Thompson were soon identified as the main suspects, and under police questioning later admitted their guilt. As soon as their identity, and more importantly their age, hit the headlines, massive public outrage erupted.

How could boys so young possibly become killers? Were they innately evil or products of their deprived backgrounds? These fundamental issues were debated endlessly in the media, and waves of hatred and revulsion washed across the entire investigation. Numerous death threats were made against the boys and their families and both their mothers were abused and threatened in the streets.

The boys were both found guilty and sentenced to prison, eventually being released in June 2001, when they were both eighteen years old. They were given new identities and sent to secret locations to begin the rest of their lives.

> In their young lives Venables and Thompson had learned that the world was a tough place where few people cared and no mercy was shown.

The Waco Incident

Vernon Howell was born in 1959 in Houston, Texas to a young single mother and raised by his grandparents in what he later described as an unhappy and lonely childhood. Having tried his hand at carpentry and rock music, as a young man he joined a rather obscure religious sect called the Branch Davidians, a group which had broken away from the mainstream Seventh Day Adventist Church.

In 1990 Howell changed his name to David Koresh. By this time he was leading a large faction of the Davidians, whose headquarters complex was located at Mount Carmel, not far from Waco in Texas. Mount Carmel was named after the biblical Mount Carmel in Israel.

The group began attracting bad publicity, with local newspaper articles alleging that Koresh was abusing his position as leader by sexually molesting children under his charge. There were also rumours that weapons were being stockpiled at the complex. Koresh was depicted as a deranged Jim Jones-style cult leader, although former members of his group later refuted this description.

Reacting mainly to the rumours about a weapons cache, officers from the Bureau of Alcohol, Tobacco and Firearms (ATF) raided the Mount Carmel complex on 28 February 1993, with a disastrous gunfight erupting soon after their attempted entry. Four ATF agents, along with six Davidians, were killed by gunfire. The ATF was forced to retreat from the scene and the FBI took over the operation.

When telephone contact was established between the authorities and Koresh, the FBI learned there were over eighty men, women and children inside the compound. Lengthy negotiations commenced to try and resolve the situation. However, a bizarre standoff developed, with the two sides unable to reach agreement on how to end the confrontation. The FBI settled in for what was to be a prolonged stay.

Days and then weeks passed, with the FBI bombarding the compound with loudspeaker messages in an attempt to unnerve the Davidians,

but to no avail. They remained in telephone contact with Koresh, who repeatedly asked for more time so that he could finish writing some religious documents before surrendering. After fifty-one days, however, the patience of the authorities ran out.

On 19 April, the FBI stormed the compound, attempting to flush the inmates out with tear gas, but this proved ineffective. Not long afterwards, flames were seen erupting from some of the buildings, and the blaze quickly spread through the complex.

The compound was consumed in flames, with all 85 Branch Davidians inside, including Koresh himself and the women and children, dying in the conflagration. The country was shocked by the terrible death toll, with many people surprised and outraged that a standoff had degenerated into a situation of mass death.

The FBI was adamant that the fire had been lit by the Davidians themselves, but this was disputed by others, and numerous conspiracy theories were spawned that remain alive today. No satisfactory explanation has ever surfaced as to why the Davidians had armed themselves and been prepared to kill, then apparently chosen to die en masse when many could have escaped the fire.

Looking back, with the benefit of hindsight, there are many who believe that the issue could have been resolved without the terrible death toll that eventuated, but history determined otherwise.

Some Davidians believe that Koresh will return to earth some time in the future, and are maintaining a vigil until that day arrives.

The group began attracting bad
publicity, with local newspaper articles
alleging that Koresh was abusing
his position as leader by sexually
molesting children under his charge.

*The Branch Davidian compound is consumed in flames, 19 April 1993 (above) as David Koresh's
grandmother talks to the press.*

Beginning in the capital, Kigali, a wave of violence fanned out across the countryside, the Hutu attacking and slaughtering Tutsis at every opportunity, encouraged, aided and abetted by both the Government and the military forces.

The remains of numerous Tutsis murdered in a church at Ntarama, Rwanda.

Genocide in Rwanda

Ethnic conflict is nothing new in Africa, being a modern offshoot of the ancient tribal warfare that has flared sporadically for centuries, long before colonial times began.

Rwanda in east-central Africa has a long history of conflict of various degrees between the two main ethnic groups, the Tutsi and the Hutu. It was once the northern part of Ruanda-Urundi, formerly a German colony, a mandated territory under Belgian administration from 1923, then a United Nations trust territory, still under Belgian administration, from 1946.

The period under Belgian administration fanned the disagreements between the Tutsi and the Hutu into a situation of escalating warfare that culminated in one of the worst mass killings of modern times. The Belgians regarded the minority Tutsi as the superior people and afforded them preferential treatment in the form of better education and employment. This generated growing resentment among the Hutu majority, who were mostly poor agriculturists and saw themselves as oppressed, and in 1959 a series of major Hutu riots led to an estimated 20 000 Tutsi being killed and possibly 150 000 more fleeing to neighbouring countries.

In 1962, Ruanda–Urundi became the independent nations of Rwanda and Burundi. A militaristic Hutu faction seized power in Rwanda, the Tutsi becoming the oppressed minority for many years. However, a large number of the Tutsi who had earlier escaped to Uganda had long planned a comeback, and formed the Rwandan Patriotic Front (RPF), which was also supported by some of the more moderate Hutus. The RPF's long-term aim was to oust the Hutu regime and return to their country.

The flashpoint came on 6 April 1994 when an aircraft carrying the Rwandan President, Juvenal Habyarimana, was shot down in a rocket attack. The President, together with several senior staff members, was killed, and the RPF was blamed. Immediate and massive Hutu reprisals against the Tutsi erupted across the country.

Beginning in the capital, Kigali, a wave of violence fanned out across the countryside, the Hutu attacking and slaughtering Tutsis at every opportunity, encouraged, aided and abetted by both the Government and the military forces. A Hutu militia of some 30 000 men was formed, and continued the program of mass murders across the countryside. A small force of United Nations peacekeeping soldiers present at the time was not authorised to intervene, and most were evacuated to safety shortly after the slaughter began.

Soon afterwards, the RPF hit back and began organised attacks on the Government forces, but they were unable to halt, or even slow down the killing. Thousands of Tutsis, as well as moderate Hutus, were being murdered every week, but the United Nations—and the world—remained reluctant to intervene in what was seen as an 'internal matter', to be solved by the country itself. In the meantime, thousands of corpses rotted in the open where they fell, in the streets of Kigali and throughout the country.

It is estimated that between April and June 1994, about 800 000 Rwandans, most of them Tutsi, were killed, and thousands more had fled the country as refugees. It was one of the worst cases of genocide ever perpetrated in the post-war world.

On 3 July 1994 the Rwandan Government collapsed, allowing the RPF to gain power and finally put an end to the bloodshed. The change of power precipitated another mass exodus of refugees, this time some two million Hutus, fearful of retribution.

On 19 July 1994, a new government was formed with both Hutu and Tutsi representatives, and promised a safe return for all Rwandans who had fled the country.

The west side of the Alfred P Murrah building devastated by the blast.

The Oklahoma Bombing

Just after nine o'clock on the morning of 19 April 1995, a normal workday was getting under way at the Alfred P. Murrah Federal building in Oklahoma City. The numerous government offices situated in the building opened up for business, and a day-care centre located on the ground floor also opened, with many children already at play inside.

In the street just outside the building, a rented Ryder truck was parked by the kerbside. From it, a few minutes earlier, a tall, angular man had been seen striding away.

Suddenly, with no warning (which is often given before a bombing), the truck virtually vaporised as an appallingly powerful explosion shook the neighbourhood for blocks around. The entire front of the nine-storey Murrah building peeled away and collapsed into the street, sending a huge cloud of dust and debris high into the air.

Incredulous rescuers converged on a scene of utter devastation and tragedy. One hundred and sixty-seven people had died in the blast, including men and women from the Federal offices and children from the child-care centre. Amid terrible scenes of pain and grief, a massive investigation was launched to determine what had happened.

Less than two hours later, some good, basic police work netted a suspect some 120 kilometres away. A highway patrolman had pulled over a motorist for not displaying a licence plate, to discover that the driver was also carrying an unlawful firearm. He was promptly arrested and jailed, awaiting a court hearing. In the meantime, evidence linking his description with that of the man who had rented the Ryder truck became available. The suspect's name was Timothy McVeigh.

Experts reconstructing the event found that the truck at the front of the building had been packed with a massive quantity of explosives that included an estimated 2300 kilograms of the fertiliser ammonium nitrate, and a quantity of nitro-methane, a highly volatile compound used in motor racing fuel. The two together produced a devastating explosion, triggered, the experts believed, by the man seen leaving the scene a few minutes earlier, perhaps by activating some sort of time-fuse.

Following further detailed forensic investigations, McVeigh, a decorated Gulf War veteran, was charged with the bombing and committed for trial. Eventually found guilty, he was sentenced to death, finally being executed on 11 June 2001, having refused to take up the full appeal process available to him. He was thirty-three years old at the time.

The reasons given for McVeigh's attack were numerous, but were believed to have stemmed from an increasing anti-government stance, and his belief that he was a freedom fighter striking a blow for the common man. This could have explained his decision to bomb a Federal Government building. He was also bitterly opposed to any form of gun control and was said to have been outraged with way the Government had handled the Branch Davidian affair in Waco, Texas, back in 1993. McVeigh had actually been there at the time and spoken to a reporter about his anger. In fact, the date of the bombing, 19 April, was two years to the day after the eighty-five Davidians were killed in the disastrous fire that consumed their compound.

> Suddenly, with no warning…the truck virtually vaporised as an appallingly powerful explosion shook the neighbourhood for blocks around.

The Bosnian Genocide

The 'Bosnian War' was a particularly brutal conflict. It was part of the break up of Yugoslavia in the early 1990s, an event that completely dominated the European political landscape of the time.

In 1992 the republic of Bosnia and Herzegovina moved to become an independent state, creating almost instant turmoil in the area. Within Bosnia there was a mixed population of Croats, Serbs and Slavs, all of whom had strong religious differences.

The Croats are predominantly Catholic, the Serbs are primarily followers of the Orthodox Church, and the Slavs are mainly Muslim. The Serbs were a minority group within Bosnia and, apparently due to their fear of being overrun in the march toward independence, began to aggressively promote their cause. Allegedly supported by the former Yugoslav leader Slobodan Milosevic, the Bosnian Serbs developed powerful paramilitary forces and began attacking both the Croats and Muslims within the Bosnian capital of Sarajevo.

The conflict escalated and continued to spread across the area for the next three years, before culminating in the infamous massacre in the Bosnian silver-mining town of Srebrenica in July 1995. Despite the United Nations (UN) maintaining a peacekeeping force in the area and establishing local 'safety zones' for civilians, the Bosnian Serbs captured Srebrenica in early July. They resolved to exact revenge for the killing of Serbs in the surrounding villages over the previous weeks, supposedly the work of the Muslim warlord Naser Oric, aided and abetted by the Muslim men of Srebrenica.

With the UN forces unable or unwilling to intervene, the Serbs rounded up the Muslim population and separated the men and boys from the women and younger children. Many other Muslim families tried to escape the situation by fleeing into the surrounding countryside, and some were successful. Over the next 5 days, from 11 to 16 July, the Serbs slaughtered over 8000 men and boys, forcing many to first dig their own graves.

Hundreds were reportedly shot at a local football field and buried nearby in huge mass graves. Serb forces then hunted down many men who had fled to the hills and ruthlessly cut them down. In an intercepted radio transmission, one of the Serb commanders was alleged to have given the order 'You must kill everyone. We don't need anyone alive'.

In what became the worst atrocity in Europe since World War II, the role of the UN forces was reduced to that of 'spectator'. Being lightly armed and heavily outnumbered by the Serbs, the terrible events unfolded before them, and the slaughter proceeded without any kind of international resistance. The Secretary General of the UN, Kofi Annan, would later remark that the failure of the UN to prevent the catastrophe would 'haunt our history forever'.

News of the massacre attracted international condemnation and the event was later ruled to be a case of genocide by the International Criminal Tribunal for the former Yugoslavia (ICTY).

The Serbs claimed that the scale of the event had been greatly exaggerated but eventually their wartime leaders, Radovan Karadzic and Ratko Mladic, were charged by the UN War Crimes Tribunal with committing genocide.

In 2003, after several of the mass burial sites had been identified, hundreds of the victims were exhumed and reburied in a special cemetery on the outskirts of Srebrenica, amid emotional scenes involving thousands of relatives of the dead.

On 26 February 2007, in a long-awaited judgement, the UN International Court of Justice ruled that Serbia had failed to restrain the Bosnian Serb Army to prevent the massacre, but that Serbia was not directly responsible for genocide.

With the UN forces unable or unwilling to intervene, the Serbs rounded up the Muslim population and separated the men and boys from the women and younger children.

The remains of victims of the Bosnian War are examined by a forensic investigator.

Floral tributes line the footpaths outside the school four days after the shootings.

The Dunblane Kindergarten Massacre

Soon after 9.15 am on Wednesday 13 March 1996, 43-year-old Thomas Hamilton, a former shopkeeper and Boy Scout leader, walked into Dunblane Primary School in the town of the same name within the rugged Perthshire Highlands of central Scotland.

Hamilton was heavily armed, carrying four handguns and a large quantity of ammunition. He began firing his weapons indiscriminately as he crossed the playground, then made his way to the school gymnasium where a class of mainly of five- and six-year-olds was having its first lesson of the day.

He began blasting away inside the building, aiming carefully at the terrified children and its teacher, Gwen Mayor. Over a maniacal three-minute period, Hamilton killed fifteen children and the teacher, before placing the muzzle of one of his handguns in his mouth and blowing the top of his head off. Another fifteen children and three adults were wounded in the rampage, with one of the children dying later in hospital.

Local police and ambulance officers swarmed into the school and were horrified by the bloody scene within the gymnasium, made all the more terrible by the fact that nearly all the victims were young children.

Scotland went into mourning. Much of the wider world reacted with shock and outrage at the enormity of the crime. Extensive investigations were immediately launched into the background of Thomas Hamilton in attempts to arrive at any possible reason to explain the insane and murderous attack.

A disturbing picture of the man soon emerged. Hamilton had previously been a Boy Scout leader, but was forced out of the movement after complaints were made about his conduct with the young boys. He later set up his own boys' club, but rumours of inappropriate behaviour surfaced there as well. Hamilton always vigorously denied any wrongdoing and became increasingly embittered at what he complained of as persecution; he claimed that a personal vendetta was being waged against him. He wrote numerous letters to the authorities in an attempt to rejoin the scouting movement, but was always rejected, adding to his frustration and growing paranoia.

His shopkeeping business collapsed—he claimed it was because of the rumours circulating about him, some of which strongly hinted at perversion and paedophilia. However, he was well accepted in one group—the local gun club scene, where he was an active practising member and holder of an official gun licence.

It was later rumoured that some local police had become concerned about what appeared to be Hamilton's 'unstable personality' and were against his continued owning of the gun licence, but because there was no actual proof that he had offended, the licence was never revoked.

It could not be established whether Hamilton had planned the carnage in advance or had 'snapped' on the morning in question, but it seemed that the tragedy had occurred because a deranged individual had access to firearms. This, in turn, sparked off considerable debate about gun ownership, not just in Scotland but across the whole of Britain, with a massive anti-gun movement mobilised.

The 'Snowdrop Petition', organised by friends of some of the victims' parents, attracted over 700 000 signatures, and eventually led to the banning of handguns right across Britain. To many this was the only good outcome from the appalling loss of young lives.

Floral tributes piled outside Kensington Palace on 2 September 1997.

The Death of Diana

Diana, Princess of Wales, was almost certainly the most recognised woman of her time. Her charisma and good looks, and her status as a member of the British Royal family made her the favourite of millions right around the world—truly a celebrity Royal.

She had married Britain's Crown Prince Charles in 1981 in a fairytale marriage ceremony that was telecast around the world, and soon became a favourite with the mass media, especially in the genre of women's magazines, where the appetite for photographs and stories about her was insatiable. When her two children were born, Prince William in 1982 and Prince Henry in 1984, they too generated a degree of media interest that continues to the present day.

Diana was in no way a non-performing Royal—she worked hard for several charities, using her tremendous drawing power as a potent marketing tool. She was particularly active in programs to secure the banning of landmines around the world, as well as assisting victims of the AIDS epidemic. This further enhanced her popularity, and some believe that during the 1980s she became the most photographed woman in world history.

In the early 1990s, however, cracks began to appear in the façade of the Camelot-type existence of Charles and Diana, with allegations of a deteriorating marriage and infidelity creeping into the gossip columns. It became increasingly obvious that the marriage was about to fail, and divorce followed in 1996. This did nothing to decrease the media demand for 'Lady Di' stories, and she continued to be pursued by the world's photographers—the paparazzi—wherever she went. Her subsequent love affair with the Egyptian millionaire Dodi Fayed was reported at length in the tabloid press, under such headlines as 'Dodi Dotes on Disi', with the British public eager to read every possible detail.

In the early 1990s, cracks began to appear in the façade of the Camelot-type existence of Charles and Diana, with allegations of a deteriorating marriage and infidelity creeping into the gossip columns.

Late on 30 August 1997, Diana was dining with Dodi at the Hotel Ritz in Paris. They left soon after midnight, accompanied by Fayed's bodyguard and their driver. The party entered a Mercedes S280 car—a luxury vehicle capable of high speed—and took off towards the underpass running beneath the Place de l'Alma. They were pursued by several French photographers, all trying to secure a Diana photograph that was worth so much to the world's newspapers.

In an attempt to escape the paparazzi, the driver accelerated to what was later claimed to be a speed around 190 kilometres an hour before the car entered the underpass. Then disaster struck. The Mercedes clipped the right side tunnel wall and careered onwards before smashing head-on into a concrete pillar. Dodi Fayed and the driver were killed on impact; Diana and the bodyguard were removed from the wreckage, still alive but severely injured.

Diana, suffering from massive internal trauma, was pronounced dead at around 4 am, and a disbelieving world plunged into an unparalleled outpouring of public grief. Six days later a massive public funeral was held at Westminster Abbey, with an estimated three million people lining the streets of London, and watched on television by a vast international audience.

Although conspiracy theories abounded following the accident, investigations showed that the driver, Diana and Dodi were not wearing seatbelts at the time of impact, and therefore had little chance of survival. The only survivor, the bodyguard, had fastened his seatbelt before the smash.

The Sydney to Hobart Race Fleet Decimated

At 1 pm sharp on 26 December 1998, the starter's gun boomed across Sydney Harbour and 115 yachts began the annual Sydney to Hobart Yacht Race in sparkling summer conditions and a gusty north-easterly sea breeze.

Followed by the large spectator fleet that traditionally accompanies the racing yachts as far as the entrance to the harbour, some 1135 sailors began the 1000 kilometre ocean race to Hobart, Tasmania, recognised as one of the world's blue water classics.

The race, held under the auspices of the Cruising Yacht Club of Australia (CYC), follows the eastern Australian coastline down to the Victorian border near Gabo Island, then across the notoriously changeable waters of Bass Strait, followed by the run down the east coast of Tasmania and finally the last leg up the Derwent River into Hobart.

The weather forecast for the race, issued by the Bureau of Meteorology (BOM) several hours before the start, and passed on to the competitors by the CYC, had indicated that a strong southerly change was developing, and a gale warning had been issued for waters over much of the course. However, soon after the start, a computer weather simulation that had just become available indicated the explosive development of an intense low-pressure cell virtually right on the track of the race.

The BOM meteorologists monitoring the situation immediately upgraded the existing gale warning to a storm warning, the first ever issued in the 51-year history of the event. A storm warning is the second highest category wind warning surpassed only by a hurricane warning. This was distributed to the CYC, and from there to the fleet, but the descent into the developing maelstrom had already begun.

As the yachts moved southwards down the coast the weather progressively deteriorated, with the wind and sea steadily rising. The leading yachts began to encounter storm-force conditions about eighteen hours into the race, with winds averaging around 50 knots (93 kph) and gusting to as high as 75 knots (139 kph). The conditions peaked across eastern Bass Strait, as the low-pressure cell predicted by the simulation intensified and smashed right through the fleet, creating havoc.

For many competitors, the notion of racing was abandoned as their situation became a straight-out fight for survival in the mountainous seas and shrieking winds. Most of the yachtsmen had never seen seas like it.

Numerous yachts were forced to retire and several crewmen were injured after being flung about their vessels. Ultimately, 55 sailors were saved from the mountainous seas through a huge rescue operation involving the Australian Maritime Safety Authority, the Navy and the Air Force. Particularly heroic efforts were performed by helicopter crews who winched sailors to safety in the incredibly dangerous flying conditions, the pilots actually manoeuvring their choppers below and between the moving crests of the massive swells. In the end, five boats sank, 66 retired and only 44 made it to the finish line. Most tragically of all, six crewmen had died in the maelstrom.

> As the yachts moved southwards down the coast the weather progressively deteriorated, with the wind and sea steadily rising.

Spectator craft follow one of the competitors soon after leaving Sydney Harbour.

The start of the 1998 Sydney to Hobart Yacht Race took place under ideal conditions.

Parents gather outside Columbine High School when it reopened four months after the shootings.

Columbine High School Massacre

Tuesday 20 April 1999 appeared to be just another day at Columbine High School in Denver, Colorado, with students beginning to gather for lunch in the school cafeteria soon after 11am. However, it was to be anything but a normal day, for it would see the second most deadly school mass murder in US history, surpassed only by the horrific Bath massacre of 1927, in which 45 people died.

Two disaffected seniors, Eric Harris and Dylan Klebold, had planted two large propane bombs in duffel bags inside the cafeteria, linked to crude timing devices set to go off soon after 11.15 am. Harris and Klebold, both heavily armed, waited outside the cafeteria, planning to shoot down those trying to flee the scene following the explosion.

However, their timing devices were faulty and the bombs failed to detonate, so the two youths decided to enter the school buildings and kill as many people as they could with the weapons they carried, which included a collection of pipe bombs.

They walked up to the school buildings, shooting at anyone who crossed their path, killing and wounding several students before entering the west entrance of the school. Then they stalked the school corridors, randomly blasting away with shotguns and automatic weapons, attempting to kill anyone they encountered. Teacher Dave Sanders was shot in the chest—later dying in a nearby room—and terrified staff and students fled or attempted to hide as the cracks of gunfire approached.

In the school library, teacher Patti Nielson was hiding with fifty-five students, all concealing themselves as best they could under desks, behind doors and in cupboards. Just before 11.30 am Harris and Klebold swung the library doors open and walked in. A dreadful series of events ensued as the shooters strolled about the library, taunting the terrified students and

every now and then stopping to blast away, killing ten more before leaving the scene. After several minutes more spent wandering about the school, Harris and Klebold returned to the library, where they both committed suicide with single gunshots to the head. The deadly rampage was over.

The Columbine shootings became instant worldwide news. Far-reaching investigations were launched to work out why the massacre had taken place, and how it could have been possible. Many facts and theories were offered in attempts to explain the tragedy.

It was alleged that Harris and Klebold had been the victims of prolonged bullying by the 'jocks', the ruling class of sports stars that supposedly dominated the less physical students at the school. It also emerged that Harris was being treated for depression, taking a drug called Luvox to ease his condition. Some theories attempted to link the taking of the anti-depressant with the outbursts of violence that Harris supposedly demonstrated from time to time.

It emerged that Harris and Klebold had minor criminal records, having attended a diversion program as a result of petty thefts committed in 1998, about a year before the shootings. It was also suggested that they had been desensitised to violence through their repeated exposure to violent music lyrics, videos and computer games, in particular the game 'Doom', in which both were regular participants.

Crash of the Concorde

In the early 1960s, airline executives around the world were busy planning the next generation of commercial passenger-carrying jet aircraft. There were two main ways to go—size or speed—and an almost infinite number of compromises in between.

The Americans eventually decided that size was the answer, and designed the largest jet ever built—the magnificent Boeing 747 Jumbo that was capable of carrying over four hundred people at around 890 kilometres an hour, resulting in an average flying time from Paris to New York of just under eight hours.

The English and French went for speed, and combined to produce the world's first super-sonic jet passenger aircraft, the fabulous Concorde. It could carry only a hundred passengers, but at a speed more than twice as fast as the Jumbo, and could travel between Paris and New York in only 3 hours and 45 minutes. Despite this dazzling performance, the cost per passenger was far greater than on the 747, taking the Concorde into the luxury end of the international air travel market.

It is history now that the 747 was by far the better commercial proposition, with the general public preferring the lower prices and increased passenger room the big jet could offer. The Concorde, however, satisfied a niche market catering for the rich and famous and for senior businessmen whose time was expensive and who needed to get to their destination as fast as possible.

Commercial flights of the Concorde began in 1976, with the aircraft's highly distinctive delta wing and dart-like appearance quickly making it a firm favourite with plane spotters around the world. Only British Airways and Air France ever purchased the aircraft, but it became a fixture on the transatlantic route over the next twenty-five years.

On 25 July 2000, disaster struck. Air France Flight 4590 was preparing to take off from Charles de Gaulle airport in Paris, outward bound for New York. As the big jet thundered down the runway, approaching lift-off speed, it hit a piece of metal lying on the tarmac. This punctured one of the tyres, and rubber debris, exploding outwards at high speed, pierced the nearby fuel tank, which immediately burst into flames.

Travelling much too fast to apply the brakes, the pilot was forced to take off, the aircraft struggling into the air and towing behind it a monstrous and ever-growing plume of fire, like a giant rocket. The crew tried to nurse the wounded jet across to nearby Le Bourget Airport, but were soon forced to shut down two of the four engines as fire engulfed them.

Unable to maintain airspeed, the Concorde gradually lost height and crashed to earth in a terrible fireball, killing all 109 people aboard, as well as four people on the ground. The last dramatic seconds of the flight were caught by amateur cameramen who happened to be passing as the aircraft flew by in its death throes.

Following the disaster, modifications were made to the construction of the Concorde, including burst-resistant tyres and puncture-proof fuel tanks, allowing services to recommence in September 2001. However, with the general drop in air travel following 9/11, combined with the escalating cost of servicing an ageing high performance aircraft, the Concorde was retired in 2003, ending, temporarily at least, the era of the supersonic passenger jet.

> As the big jet thundered down the runway, approaching lift-off speed, it hit a piece of metal lying on the tarmac.

A magnificent view of the Concorde under full power on take-off.

The Sinking of the *Kursk*

The Russian submarine *Kursk* was a massive vessel, over 150 metres in length, of a heavy-duty double-hulled construction that was considered totally unsinkable. A nuclear-powered cruise-missile submarine of the Oscar II type, the *Kursk* was capable of travelling vast distances and of staying submerged for more than three months at a time while remaining virtually undetectable.

A cornerstone of the Russian Northern Fleet, the *Kursk* was launched in 1994, and had proved its worth as a secret reconnaissance vessel in 1999, when it successfully shadowed the US Navy's Sixth Fleet during the Kosovo War. Carrying the latest top secret Russian Navy weaponry, including twelve SS-N-19 Shipwreck missiles, each capable of sinking an enemy aircraft carrier, the *Kursk* was a formidable fighting machine.

A large-scale naval exercise had been planned for the Russian Northern Fleet in the Barents Sea during August 2000, with the *Kursk* one of four attack submarines involved, accompanied by a large force of aircraft carriers, cruisers and destroyers. This represented a revival for the Russian Navy, which had been subjected to significant financial cutbacks over the previous decade, with funds insufficient to keep a large part of its fighting fleet in operational mode.

One of the *Kursk*'s roles was to stage a mock attack on a nearby battlecruiser, firing a series of dummy torpedoes to simulate the attack. This was launched at around 11.30 am on 12 August—and disaster followed. A gigantic explosion ripped through the forward part of the submarine, tearing a large gash through both the twin steel hulls and sending the vessel plunging to the ocean bed in some 108 metres of water, with 118 sailors trapped inside.

Alarmed at possible world reaction to a nuclear submarine accident, Russian authorities did not release news of the disaster for more that twenty-four hours, hoping to mount a rescue mission without having to call in outside assistance. It is probable that they were also motivated by the fact that much of the weaponry and associated instrumentation aboard the *Kursk* was top secret and therefore not for viewing by outsiders.

Two days later, on 14 August, they finally admitted to the incident, saying only that the *Kursk* had 'malfunctioned' and that a Russian rescue effort was well under way. Assistance was requested from NATO the next day, after an initial rescue attempt had apparently failed. As further rescue attempts proved futile, Russia's citizens increasingly criticised the national leadership for its slow reaction, fearing that if there were men still alive aboard the *Kursk* their time was running out because of slow-moving officialdom. On Friday 18 August, wives and mothers of the sailors heckled and abused the Russian Deputy Prime Minister at a meeting in Severomorsk. Finally, on 21 August, some nine days after the explosion, British and Norwegian divers succeeded in opening the submarine's rear escape hatches, to find the entire vessel flooded. There was no hope of finding any survivors, and all 118 crewmen were officially declared lost.

In October 2001, over a year following the disaster, the *Kursk* was raised by a Dutch salvage company and towed to nearby Roslyakovo drydock. The bodies of 115 of the 118 sailors were recovered from the wreck and laid to rest, ending one of Russia's worst peacetime disasters.

> A gigantic explosion ripped through the submarine, sending the vessel plunging to the ocean bed with 118 sailors trapped inside.

The mother of a Kursk sailor is comforted by a Russian seaman at a memorial ceremony in Vidyayevo.

Russian television films a rescue capsule being lowered to be sent to the Kursk submarine.

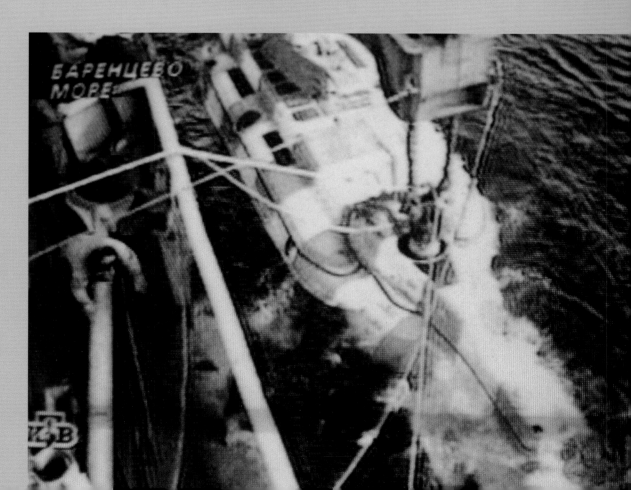

A Ford Explorer vehicle equipped with Firestone tyres prior to the recall.

Ford vs Firestone

In the late 1990s a worrying series of accidents across the United States began plaguing the popular Ford Explorer, eventually resulting in an estimated 250 deaths and many more serious injuries. The problem appeared to involve tread separation in the Firestone tyres that came as standard equipment with the Explorer. This sometimes occurred at speed on a freeway, when the tread peeled off the main body of the tyre, producing loss of control followed by vehicle rollover.

In May 2000, the US National Highway Traffic Safety Administration (NHTSA) asked both Ford and Firestone for an explanation. This triggered one of the greatest ructions seen in the automobile industry since the publication of Ralph Nader's book *Unsafe at Any Speed* way back in 1965. Following detailed research, the two companies returned to NHTSA's conference table each claiming to know the root cause of the accidents—the other company.

Firestone maintained that there was no fault in their tyres, but that Ford's recommended tyre pressures for the Explorer were too low; Firestone also maintained that the vehicle contained inherent design problems that made it unstable, particularly in the event of a tyre failure.

Ford, on the other hand, believed that there was a manufacturing problem with the Firestone tyres fitted on the Explorer, particularly those made at Firestone's plant in Decatur, Illinois, which was causing the tread separation behind the rollovers. In support of this argument, Ford noted that Goodyear tyres fitted to the Ford Explorer had not produced similar problems.

The rift between Firestone and Ford was particularly painful for all concerned, as the relationship between the two companies had been longstanding and friendly, with Firestone being the preferred tyre provider for most of the Ford models all the way back to the Model T in 1908. However, with so much at stake, both financially and in the area of worldwide public credibility, the companies went into battle against each other hammer and tongs.

Claim and counter-claim followed, with the two companies slugging it out in the media, hoping to gain some points in the public relations war before NHTSA released its official report. In mid-2000, Ford announced that it would replace some 6.5 million Firestone tyres on its vehicles; then, with the problems allegedly persisting, planned a further massive recall in May of 2001. Firestone pre-empted this move by announcing that it would no longer supply tyres to Ford, with CEO John Lampe remarking, 'Business relationships, like personal ones, are built upon trust and mutual respect. We have come to the conclusion that we can no longer supply tyres to Ford since the basic foundation of our relationship has been seriously eroded.'

In late 2001, the long-awaited NHTSA report was issued. It apportioned most of the blame for the problem to Firestone, with Ford immediately claiming victory in the increasingly ugly conflict. Firestone refused to concede, however, saying that it disagreed with the official findings and maintained that their tyres were safe. They did, however, agree to the further tyre recall recommended by the NHTSA.

Multiple lawsuits were launched by crash victims against both Ford and Firestone over the issue, producing a mixture of results, with a number settled out of court. The cost to Ford and Firestone is unknown, but some observers believe that it must have run into many millions of dollars for both companies.

United Airlines Flight 175 slams into the World Trade Center south tower.

9/11

The morning of 11 September 2001 was fine and clear across New York City, with people out and about in the streets, and office workers just beginning their routine for the day.

At 8.47 am, and literally out of the blue, people in the street below the north tower of the World Trade Center were witness to the utterly surrealistic sight of a large jet aircraft crashing into the upper levels of the building. A great gush of flame erupted, followed by a growing plume of black smoke that stained the blue skies over the city.

About sixteen minutes later, the large crowds that had gathered to watch the incident were astounded to see a second jet rapidly approaching. To their utter amazement, it slammed into the south tower of the World Trade Center. A second huge explosion and fireball rocked the area, generating another plume of smoke.

Just before 9.38 am, word came in that a third aircraft had crashed into the Pentagon in Washington DC and, a little later, a fourth into a field in Pennsylvania. A worldwide television audience watched in disbelief as, one after the other, the two 110-storey World Trade Center towers, now well ablaze in their upper portions, shuddered, and collapsed in a giant pall of dust.

With the realisation that a coordinated attack had just been launched against the United States, the biggest peacetime investigation in history was immediately launched. The FBI and CIA were fully mobilised, and it didn't take long to reveal a plot that would have been considered almost too fantastic for a Hollywood movie.

It was discovered that a group of nineteen young Arab men associated with the terror group al-Qaeda had been living and training in the United States, specifically planning for this operation. Several had paid large sums of money for pilot training at a flying school, and it was alleged that the finances behind them originated from al-Qaeda.

On the morning of September 11 they had boarded four commercial jet airliners, two taking off from Boston, one from New Jersey and the other from Washington DC. Soon after takeoff the hijackers took over the four aircraft, killing a number of passengers and crew with box-cutters they had smuggled aboard. The flight decks were invaded and the flight crews either overpowered or killed, allowing the hijackers to take control of the aircraft.

The big Boeing jets were diverted at top speed to their pre-arranged targets, the World Trade Center towers and the Pentagon. It was theorised that the aircraft that crashed in Pennsylvania could have been intended for the White House, but that passengers had fought the hijackers and thwarted the operation.

Nearly 3,000 people died in the attacks, but the effects went much further than the immediate death toll. The event produced the realisation that terrorism, for decades an element of political activism in the Middle East, was now a global issue, and no country was immune.

Internal security across the United States, and indeed in much of the world, was tightened considerably, including all forms of air travel and shipping, and there was a worldwide crackdown on money movements and travel documents.

Pronouncements from al-Qaeda following the incident indicated that the United States and all its allies were to be the targets for future attacks, with the indiscriminate killing of civilians considered legitimate retribution for past US policies. The world became a different place after 9/11.

> The FBI and CIA were fully mobilised, and it didn't take long to reveal a plot that would have been considered almost too fantastic for a Hollywood movie.

The Collapse of Enron

In the mid to late 1990s, a large energy company shone brightly as one of the crown jewels of the American corporate world. The giant Houston-based Enron was named 'America's Most Innovative Company' from 1996 to 2001 by the prestigious *Fortune* magazine, which also included Enron in its list of '100 Best Companies to Work for in America'. Employment conditions for Enron's 21 000 employees in the United States and around the world were generally fabulous, with luxurious office accommodations and top salaries.

Enron's share price on the stock exchange hit $90 in August of 2000, and annual revenue that year was projected to be a mammoth US$101 billion, making Enron, on paper, one of the most successful companies in the world at that time.

The organisation began back in 1930 as the Northern Natural Gas Company. Following a complex series of restructures and takeovers it became Enron in 1985, under a new CEO, Kenneth Lay. An innovative businessman, Lay began building up Enron's range of trading products to include far more than just the traditional energy profile. A virtual kaleidoscope of new items appeared in the Enron portfolio, ranging from power to plastics, from weather derivatives to credit risk management, from steel to broadband services.

Lay was a visionary and the company appeared to prosper under his guidance, although some of the diversifications were untried and perhaps risky. In 1999, Enron initiated the first web-based transaction system, EnronOnline, which allowed buyers and sellers to trade globally in various commodity products. This further enhanced the company's growing public reputation as an innovator and market leader.

The first chinks started to appear in this Camelot castle during the first half of 2001, when several senior Enron executives began selling large blocks

> The first chinks started to appear in this Camelot castle during the first half of 2001, when several senior Enron executives began selling large blocks of their company stock.

of their company stock. As it turned out later, the company had been trading for some time through so-called 'special purpose and offshore entities', which were basically partnerships controlled by Enron itself. This arrangement produced spectacular profits and revenue, but without any losses making their way onto the balance sheet. By the beginning of 2001, far from being the Midas 'touch of gold' company, Enron was in serious financial difficulties.

As word filtered out, Enron share prices began sliding rapidly, from a high of $90 in August 2000 to just below $47 in July 2001. Alarm bells were ringing, but investors were urged not to sell and reassured that the situation would eventually rebound. Enron executives, however, continued to sell their stock at an accelerated rate. By the end of October the share price had fallen to just $15, and investors were made even more anxious by the company's announcement that the US Securities and Exchange Commission (SEC) had initiated an official investigation into the situation.

Unable to exert control, Enron executives watched as the share price went into free fall, closing out the year at a disastrous $0.30. In early December, Enron filed for bankruptcy, finally revealing that a colossal corporate collapse had occurred. The fallout was instantaneous and massive, with several official investigations launched.

An online catalogue announces the sale of items from Enron's UK headquarters, February 2002.

Allegations of financial criminal behaviour immediately surfaced, including securities fraud, conspiracy, money laundering, insider trading and making false statements to banks and auditors. Criminal charges followed, and Enron's accounting firm, Arthur Andersen, was also implicated, triggering a further round of damaging financial investigations.

The Enron affair turned out to be the greatest corporate collapse in history up until that time, and the legal and financial fallout continued for several years.

Rescuers carry a wounded pupil to safety in the midst of the siege.

A memorial to those killed in the massacre, located in the ruins of the school gymnasium.

For several days around 25 000 people sheltered in the Louisiana Superdome; others sought refuge on the upper floors of buildings in an effort to escape the rising floodwaters.

Wreckage of all description lines the shoreline near Biloxi, Mississippi, soon after 'Katrina' had struck.

Index

O
obesity, 248
oil spill, *Exxon Valdez*, 242
Oklahoma bombings, 259
Oppenheimer, Julius, 137
Oswald, Lee Harvey, 168
ozone layer, hole in, 228

P
Palace of Knossos, 20
Pakistan, formation of, 139
Pankhurst, Emmeline, 77
Parker, Pauline, 149
Pearl Harbor, bombing of, 122
penicillin, 140
Plague, Black, 33
plastic bags, 155
Pol Pot's regime, 204
Pompeii, 25
potato famine, 54
powered flight, 116
Princess Diana's death, 265
Profumo affair, 165
Prohibition, 60, 96

R
Rainbow Warrior, bombing of, 227
Rape of Nanking, 113
Ray, James Earl, 179
Repressed Memory Syndrome, 251
Rice-Davies, Mandy, 164–5
Roman Empire, Fall of, 22–3
Rwanda, genocide in, 257

S
Salem witch hunts, 45
San Francisco earthquake, 81
self-immolation, 167
September 11, 2001, 277
Shimantan Dam collapse, 202
Singapore, Fall of, 125
Six-Day War, 177
smog, 145
smoking, 151
Spanish influenza, 95
Spanish Inquisition, 31
St Valentine's Day massacre, 96
Staphylococcus bacteria, 140
Stalin, Joseph, 100–1, 127
Stalingrad, Battle of, 127
storms, 47, 102
suffragettes, 77
Sumer, 19
Superbug (Staphylococcus), 140
Sydney to Hobart Yacht Race, 266

T
Tangshan earthquake, 209
tank warfare, 93, 128
Tasmanian tiger, 110–11
Tate, Sharon, 180
Tate–LaBianca murders, 180
Tenerife air disaster, 210
thalidomide, 161
thylacine, 110–11
Tiananmen Square, 245
Titanic, 84
tobacco, 151
tornadoes, 102
Trafalgar, Battle of, 49
Tri-State Tornado, 102
tsunamis, 66, 283
Tunguska Meteorite, 83
Typhoon Nina, 202

U
Union Carbide India Limited, 224
Unsafe at Any Speed, 174

V
V-1 and V-2 flying bombs, 133
Vietnam War, 138, 162, 167
volcanic eruptions
  Krakatoa, 66
  Mount St Helen's, 221
  Mount Tambora, 50–1
  Mount Vesuvius, 25
  Thera, 21
von Braun, Wernher, 133
von Ohain, Hans, 116

W
Waco, Texas, 254
Wall Street Crash, 107
Watergate, 196–7
Waterloo, Battle of, 53
Watts riots, 173
Whittle, Frank, 116
witch hunts, 45
World Trade Center, 276
World War I, 87–93
World War II, 109, 121–38
Wright Brothers, 79

Y
Year Without a Summer, 50–1

Z
Zola, Emile, 72